THE VICTORIA HISTORY OF GLOUCESTERSHIRE

YATE

Rose Wallis

First published 2015

A Victoria County History publication

© The University of London, 2015

ISBN 978 1 909646 10 0

Published with the generous support of South Gloucestershire Council.

Cover image: Yate shopping centre, architect's impression, *c.*1965 (reproduced by permission of Yate Heritage Centre).
Back cover image: Map: Greenwood, 1824, detail.

Typeset in Minion pro by Emily Morrell

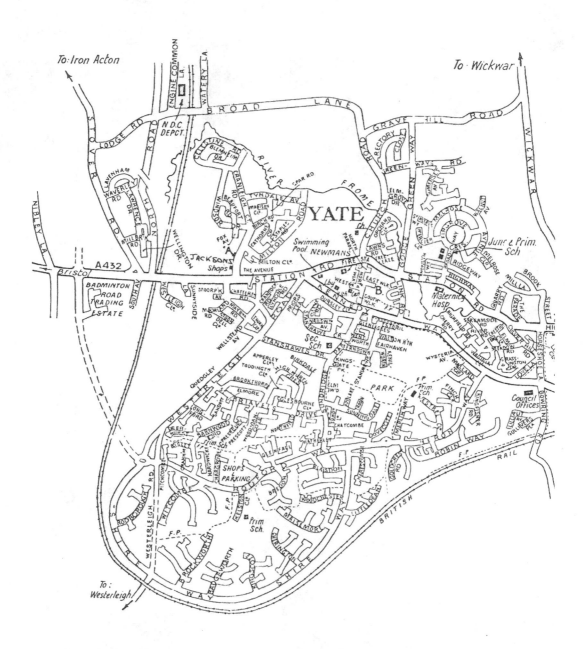

Yate urban area, street plan, 1978.

CONTENTS

LIST OF ILLUSTRATIONS

Figures are reproduced by kind permission of Yate Heritage Centre, except where credited otherwise.

Frontispiece   Yate urban area, street plan, 1978. GA, DC 93/6/3, reproduced by permission of South Gloucestershire Council.

Figure

Map

Table

FOREWORD

ANY PROJECT WHICH SETS OUT to describe every community in the county is bound to appeal to a Lord-Lieutenant, but it gives me particular pleasure to welcome this new account of Yate, the latest instalment in the long-running Victoria County History series.

Firstly, there is the intrinsic interest of Yate itself, which seems always to have had an enterprising culture, and a willingness to make the most of its resources, be they under the ground, above ground, or more importantly in the population itself. This spirit led to its becoming the first New Town in the historic county of Gloucestershire.

Secondly, given that my office embraces the whole ceremonial county, it is heartening to see the great Victoria County History enterprise finally reaching South Gloucestershire. The delay stems partly from the boundary changes of 1974, and I am glad that a mere 40 years later, we have found an amicable way forward.

Thirdly, I applaud the energy and dedication of the staff and volunteers at the Yate Heritage Centre. Without their evident enthusiasm, and the work they have already done in capturing so many aspects of what makes Yate distinctive and interesting – including oral history, some of which is quoted here – I do not think there would have been the incentive to begin this account.

This publication is of course but the first step in bringing the story of Yate and the surrounding communities to wider attention. Many more parish histories will follow, as the research proceeds. I urge any readers who like what they see in this book, and want to see more, to support the continuing work of the Gloucestershire County History Trust: its members have co-ordinated and co-funded the project.

Janet Trotter

Dame Janet Trotter
Lord-Lieutenant of Gloucestershire

ACKNOWLEDGEMENTS

THE HISTORY OF YATE PRESENTED HERE is a significant milestone for the Gloucestershire County History Trust. While draft sections have been available online since 2013, its publication in this form is a first for the Trust, and the first opportunity to record in print our thanks to a wide circle of supporters. The Trust, a registered charity, was set up in 2010 to carry forward the work of the Victoria County History in Gloucestershire, which up to that point had been funded jointly by the County Council and the University of Gloucestershire. The Trust's initial focus was on completing a volume of histories of 13 parishes in the Severn and Leadon Valleys, which had been placed on hold when public funding ceased. We remain immensely grateful to all the many individuals who rallied round in those first months. Their support was followed by that of the Bristol & Gloucestershire Archaeological Society, who made a very generous grant that gave the Trust the confidence – and the wherewithal – to recruit an experienced historian, Dr John Chandler, now County Editor, to resume the research.

This good start was made even better by the news in 2012 that South Gloucestershire Council was keen to sponsor the production of a VCH-quality history of Yate. The grant made by the Council in that year allowed us to engage a Bristol-based historian, Rose Wallis, to research Yate from the earliest times to the present day and to write up the results, under John Chandler's editorial guidance, with the results you now see. The practical support of David Hardill and colleagues at the Yate Heritage Centre has been invaluable, putting us in touch with a cadre of local volunteers who among other things made abstracts of numerous inventories, and distilled the Yate facts from the voluminous records of the 1940s agricultural survey. We look forward to continued contacts with local groups and societies as the work progresses, and this is an appropriate point to acknowledge the very welcome financial support received from the Avon Local History Association.

Similarly, we acknowledge with gratitude the unfailing and always friendly support of staff at Gloucestershire Archives, which retains responsibility for the records of the whole historic county. They have made facilities available to both the Trust's editors and the wider circle of volunteers, supporting an informal partnership of mutual benefit.

We also place on record our warm appreciation of the encouragement and continuing interest of the Honourable Company of Gloucestershire and its members, who had a short preview of this work when Rose Wallis spoke after their AGM in November 2013, and who have since helped us forge new links across the county.

Finally, the Trust records its gratitude to the VCH's hard-working central staff at the University of London, who have been responsible for overseeing the final editorial stages of this book, and arranging for its publication in this form. In due course, this history of Yate will, with any revisions arising from further research, form part of the planned Volume 14 of the Victoria County History of Gloucestershire. Besides Yate, the volume will also cover the parishes of Chipping Sodbury, Little Sodbury and Old Sodbury; and Acton Turville, Dodington, Tormarton, Wapley with Codrington, and West Littleton.

James Hodsdon

Dr James Hodsdon
Chairman, Gloucestershire County History Trust

INTRODUCTION

AS A TOWN YATE IS RELATIVELY NEW, and unknown to many; but even the most illustrious towns were new once, and they trailed a long past before their urban present. Yate has grown rapidly since the 1950s, to become the most populous town in South Gloucestershire, and the third largest, after Gloucester and Cheltenham, in the historic county.[1] And like these older centres, its earlier history, fashioned over hundreds of years by thousands of people, is inscribed in the layout of its streets, its names and boundaries, the monuments around its noble church, and in its farms whose pastures have become housing estates. Even a stroll along Station Road, Yate's workaday benchmark, reveals hints to the observant of a rich past with its rural cottages and railway hub, and of a close-knit community with a proud industrial and commercial heritage. The gentle farmland beyond the houses, the worked-out quarries and the commons – these too are vital to the long story.

Yate's name means gateway: the original gateway led into a royal forest, a place of privilege and rich resources, a world of medieval lords and bishops, and later farmers and peasants, colliers and entrepreneurs. Yate's more recent history has included industry (rare mineral extraction and aircraft production) and commerce (a pioneering shopping mall).

Today Yate is a parish within South Gloucestershire unitary authority, 45 km south-west of Gloucester, 18 km north-east of Bristol and very close to the market town of Chipping Sodbury. Administratively the parish lay within Gloucestershire until 1974, and in Avon county 1974–96.[2] Before 1900 Yate was a village of moderate size concentrated along Station Road (A 432), between Iron Acton in the west and Chipping Sodbury in the east. From c.1955 extensive urban development saw Yate reinvented as a new town.[3]

Prior to urban expansion the ancient parish extended over 4,081 a. of predominantly flat vale, bounded on the east by a ridge of carboniferous limestone.[4] Before 1228, when it was disafforested, Yate lay within Horwood forest; thereafter the manorial lords cleared their lands, enabling more extensive pastoral farming and the exploitation of rich geological and mineral deposits. Coal, sandstone, limestone and celestine (strontium sulphate) were won and worked within the parish.[5]

---

1   This account was written in 2012–14. Population totals from *Census,* 2011. By some measures Stroud and Kingswood urban areas are also larger than Yate.
2   Youngs, *Admin. Units* I, 192.
3   See pp. 54–9; 64–6.
4   OS Maps 6", Glos. LXIV.SW, LXIX.NW, SW (1886 edns); *OS Area Book* (1880); Geol. Surv. Map, 1", Bristol District, new series, special sheet (1962 edn).
5   See pp. 47–53.

Yate's diverse economy, and its proximity to Bristol's ports and urban markets, paved the way for its expansion. The railway, from 1844, and light industry after 1914, provided the economic foundation for the development of a new town in the 1960s.[6]

Parish Boundaries

The boundaries of Yate ancient parish remained largely unchanged until 1988 when, following a boundary commission review, the parish was reconfigured to reflect the town's urban development.[7] Large parts of the ancient parish, including significant portions of Yate manor, were then lost to Wickwar.[8] This account concentrates on the parish as it existed before 1988; but the urban development of the 'new town' and subsequent related changes to Yate's administrative structures are also considered.[9]

The Ancient Parish

In 1881 and 1903 the parish was computed at 4,081 a.,[10] but earlier estimates varied. An agricultural commentator in 1803 over-stated the total as 4,500 a., made up of 3,500 a. pasture, 400 a. common, and the remainder arable.[11] The 1831 census calculated 3,400 a.,[12] and the tithe commissioners' report of 1838, based on 'tolerably correct' estimates, described the parish as containing 267 a. arable, 2,447 a. pasture, and 600 a. common land, totalling 3,314 a.[13] The final apportionment, however, calculated total acreage at 4,042 a., the figure adopted by the 1851 census.[14]

These discrepancies may be attributed to the inclosure of common land in Yate and adjacent parishes. Commons bounded Yate to the west, south-west, north and north-east, flanking the parishes of Rangeworthy, Iron Acton, Westerleigh, Wickwar and Horton,[15] and 19th-century inclosure awards affecting Yate and its neighbours included several claims on portions of commons straddling Yate's borders.[16]

The northern limits of Yate parish followed the Ladden Brook, a tributary of the Frome, just south of Wickwar. Its eastern boundary, with Horton and Old Sodbury, traversed woodlands and common in its north-eastern quarter, defined by Bishop's Brook.[17] Returning to meet the southern branch of the Ladden Brook, from Brinsham, the eastern boundary followed the limestone ridge southwards, overlapping the Sodbury to Wickwar road. The Frome, flowing into the parish from the south-east and exiting in

6   See pp. 54–9.
7   Youngs, *Admin. Units* I, 192; OS Maps 6", Glos. LXIV.SW, LXIX.NW, SW (1886, 1903 edns); see pp. 64–6.
8   Northavon (Parishes) Order 1988, SI 1988/112; GA, P 357a PC 11/1/2, *Local Government Boundary Commission Report* 443, 1983, app. B.
9   See pp. 64–6.
10   OS Map 6", Glos. LXIX.NW (1903 edn); *Census*, 1881.
11   Rudge, *Hist. of Glos.* II, 367; see also Rudge, *Agric. of Glos.* (1807), 355.
12   *Census*, 1831.
13   TNA, IR 18/2952.
14   Ibid.; GDR, T 1/207; *Census, 1851.*
15   Taylor, *Map of Glos.* (1777); Greenwood, *Map of Glos.* (1824); OS Maps 1", sheet 35 (1830 edn); 6", Glos. LXIV.SW, LXIX.NW, SW (1886 edn).
16   GA, Q/RI/164; Q/RI/1; D 5886 3/1; PC 474; Q/RI/81; Q/RI/157.
17   This para: Taylor, *Map of Glos.* (1777); OS Maps 6", Glos. LXIV.SW, LXIX.NW (1886 edn); GDR, T 1/207; Q/RI/164; D 2762/T14 (1254); D 2272 (1745).

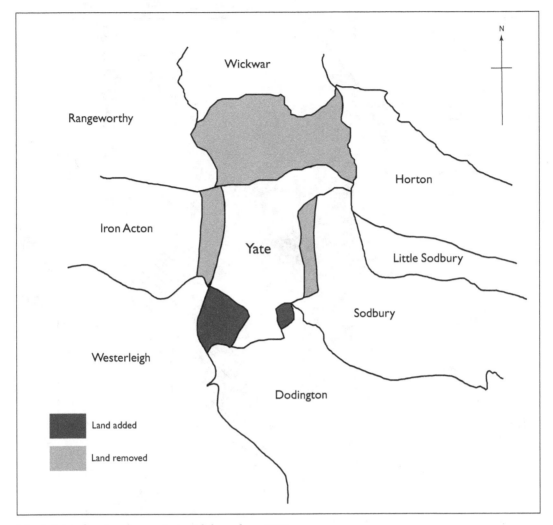

Map 1 *Map showing changes to parish boundary, 1988*

the west, divided Yate from Old Sodbury. The irregular southern parish boundary was dictated by Stanshawes manor's territory, bisecting Yate (or Eggshill) and Westerleigh Commons,[18] to meet the western boundary with Iron Acton. Following the northward extension of the 'ancient heath', or Engine Common and Yate Lower Common, it completed its western perimeter along the border with Rangeworthy.

The parish comprised three manors. Yate, the largest, was centred on Yate Court, north of Tanhouse Lane, while Brinsham occupied the east and Stanshawes the extreme south of the parish.[19] Hall End and Church End were administrative divisions by 1712.[20] Hall End encompassed the more diffusely settled area north of Tanhouse Lane, while

18   Recorded as Yate Common, 1886; Eggshill Common and Westerleigh Common, 1903.
19   See pp. 24–34.
20   GA, Q/SR/1754; Atkyns, *Glos.* I, 856–7; Rudder, *Glos.* 854–5.

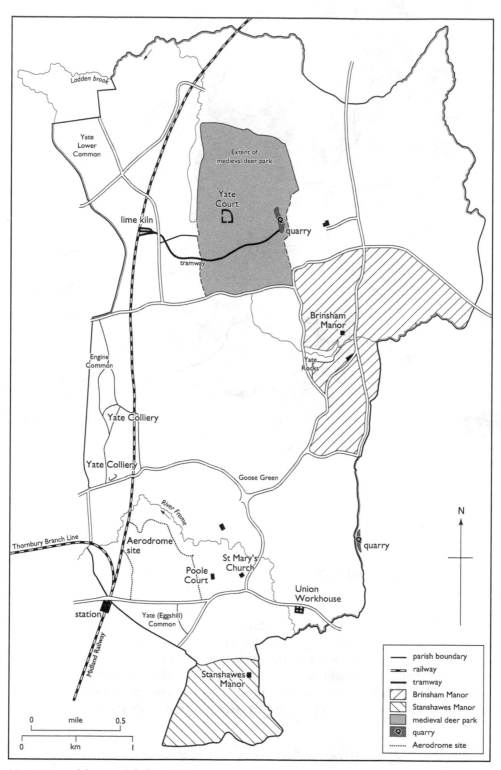

Map 2 *Map of the parish before 1988.*

Church End included the more densely populated southern half of the parish, focused on St Mary's church, along the main route from Bristol (Station Road) and the road north to Goose Green.[21] This division of the parish foreshadowed the trajectory of urban development and the consequent re-drawing of parish boundaries in 1988.

The Modern Parish

After the 1988 boundary alterations, the civil parish of Yate was reduced to 2,471 a. (1,000 ha).[22] The new boundaries reflected the now 'purely urban' character of the settlement.[23] The largely undeveloped and predominantly rural area north of Tanhouse Lane was removed to Wickwar. Land west of the railway line was transferred to Rangeworthy and Iron Acton, and much of the ridge, extending to Yate Rocks, became part of Sodbury. The historic manor of Brinsham was retained within the parish, confined by Mapleridge Road and the Ladden Brook. Areas where the urban development had encroached on adjacent parishes were generally incorporated within Yate's new boundaries, most significantly, from Westerleigh and Dodington.[24] New roads, Scott Way and Rodford Way, south of Station Road, defined the southern half of the parish.[25]

The Landscape

Yate's superficially unvaried terrain masks a complex geological sequence which has shaped it as an economically diverse settlement. Most of the ancient parish extended over a pastoral plain *c.*70 m. above sea level, part of the shallow and broad Ladden Brook valley. The Wickwar ridge formed the highest ground, extending along the eastern boundary *c.*30 m. above the valley floor, interrupted by the Ladden Brook at Yate Rocks to form a shallow escarpment.[26]

The centre and west of the ancient parish covered the northern limits of the Bristol Coal Measure. The coal seams were interspersed with and bounded by Pennant sandstone to the west. The ridge to the east was formed of Carboniferous limestone, sloping westwards into sandstone before expanding into the floor of the vale.[27] Coal was dug from 1600 or earlier, and the use of local sandstone and limestone can be seen in 17th-century and later dwellings, especially east of Yate settlement.[28]

Between the coal measure and the ridge Mercia mudstone (known also as Keuper Marl) outcrops in the centre of the parish, interspersed with small areas of gravel and alluvium around the Ladden Brook and Frome.[29] At *c.*9 m. below the red marls, deposits

21 See pp. 61–4.

22 Calculation from OS 1:25,000 sheet 167 (1998 edn).

23 GA, P 357a PC 11/1/2, *Local Government Boundary Commission Report*, 443, 1983, app. B.

24 Northavon (Parishes) Order 1988, SI 1988/112; other very small areas (shaded on map) were incorporated into Westerleigh and Dodington; OS 1:25,000, sheet 167 (1998 edn).

25 OS 1:25,000, sheet 167 (1998 edn).

26 Ibid.; S. Glos. Council, *Landscape Character Assessment* (2005), 148.

27 Geol. Surv. Map, 1", Bristol District, new series, special sheet (1962 edn).

28 Smith, *Men and Armour*, 216 lists two miners; A. Buchanan and N. Cossons, *Industrial Archaeology of the Bristol Region* (1969), 93; see below pp. 47–50.

29 Geol. Surv. Map, 1", Bristol District, new series, special sheet (1962 edn).

of celestine (strontium sulphate or spar) were excavated until the 1990s.[30] Yate's extractive industries spawned subsidiary enterprises, including the production of lime and ochre, and brickworks, which in turn led to the growth of distributive networks, significantly the railway in the 1840s.[31]

On Yate's extensive flatlands, particularly in the centre and north, farming – predominantly pastoral – continued alongside quarrying and mining into the 20th century.[32] Much of this land lay within the medieval royal forest of Horwood which, until the 13th century, extended from the outskirts of Bristol as far north as Wotton-under-Edge, and from the Severn eastwards to Old Sodbury.[33] To raise revenue, in 1228 Henry III relinquished royal privileges to all but a small area of forest close to Bristol, known as Kingswood Chase.[34] Manorial lords within the former forest, upon payment, cleared, inclosed and cultivated their lands, the process of disafforestation also encouraging the expansion of the earlier settlements.[35]

Attempts to inclose land for cultivation within Yate were first recorded in 1254.[36] Small, irregular fields, particularly in the north of the parish, suggest that this early inclosure continued,[37] so that following the regional pattern, only commons and wastes were subject to parliamentary inclosure in the 19th century.[38] Likewise, away from the north-east corner of the parish and along the limestone ridge in the south, little woodland remained after 1800;[39] although field names and archaeological evidence suggest that it was formerly more extensive in central and southern Yate, and that exploitation of woodland products contributed to the local economy.[40]

Yate's productive diversity, transport links and proximity to Bristol attracted industrial development not confined to its extractive industries. The expansion of Bristol-based large enterprises after 1900 established a basis for light industry in the parish, and the subsequent development of the new town.[41]

Communications

Roads

Two important early routes traversed Yate. What became known from the 1840s as Station Road, linking Nibley (in Westerleigh) with Chipping Sodbury across the south of

30   F. Walker, *Bristol Region* (1972), 24, 281; Buchanan and Cossons, *Ind. Arch. of Bristol Region*, 129–30; Avon CCl, *Mineral Report*, 1978; local inf.; see below pp. 51–3.

31   See pp. 8–10.

32   See pp. 45–7.

33   *Cal. Chart.* I, 75; http://info.sjc.ox.ac.uk/forests/ForestIndexSWMidlands.html (accessed 12 Jan. 2015); J. Speed, *Map of Glos.* (1611); J.S. Moore, 'Med. Forest of Kingswood', *Avon Past*, 7 (1982), 6–16; author is grateful for advance access to M.H. and J. Martin, *A History of Lower Woods Nature Reserve Part II The Timeline* (Hawkesbury Local History Society, 2014), 69–76.

34   TNA, C 60/27, m. 5, no 173; Smith, *Lives of the Berkeleys* (1883), I, 114.

35   *Cal. Chart.* I, 75; D. Brown, *Avon Heritage* (1979); Moore, 'Med. Forest of Kingswood'.

36   GA, D 2762/T14, 27 June 1254.

37   GDR, T 1/207; D 1610/E/120; Walker, *Bristol Region*, 161.

38   GA, Q/RI/164; below p. 46.

39   GDR, T 1/207.

40   GDR, T 1/207: 'Wooderys', 'Brake', 'Dingley'; Saw Pit at Yate Rocks, OS 6", Glos. LXIX.NW (1886 edn).

41   See pp. 54–9.

Figure 1 *The tollhouse situated on the Sodbury to Wickwar road at the junction with Love Lane, c.1910.*

the parish, formed a well-established route from Bristol via Cirencester to Oxfordshire in 1675.[42] A second road, running northward from Chipping Sodbury along the eastern parish boundary to Wickwar was a main thoroughfare by 1725.[43] Station Road remained the principal thoroughfare within the parish, and provided the focus for residential and commercial development in the 18th and 19th centuries.[44]

The first turnpike trust to impinge on Yate was established under an act of 1725–6, which permitted tolls to be levied for repairing and widening the roads from Gloucester to Stone, and those 'to and near Berkeley, Dursley, Wotton under Edge, Stroud, and Sodbury'.[45] The breadth and imprecision of this act were not lost on contemporaries; subsequent acts of 1746, 1758/9 and 1778/9 clarified the routes and the trusts responsible for them.[46] The road through Chipping Sodbury was turnpiked under an act of 1751/2, and formed a significant link in the network used by traffic between Wiltshire and South Wales via Aust ferry.[47] The extent of turnpike roads within the parish was explicitly stated in an act of 1799/1800, which brought both routes under the responsibility of a single trust for the Sodbury division.[48] This was amalgamated in 1849 with the Cirencester to

42   J. Ogilby, *Britannia*, I (1675), pl. 55; Taylor, *Map of Glos.* (1777); OS Maps 1", sheet 35 (1830 edn); 6", Glos. LXIX.NW, SW (1886 edn).

43   Local (Glos.) Roads Act, 12 Geo. I, c. 24; depicted on Taylor, *Map of Glos.* (1777).

44   See pp. 53–9.

45   Local (Glos.) Roads Act, 12 Geo. I, c. 24.

46   Local (Glos.) Roads Act, 31 Geo. II, c. 64; Wilts. & Glos. Roads Act,, 18 Geo. III, c. 103.

47   *VCH Wilts.* IV, 254–71.

48   Sodbury Roads Act, 39–40 Geo. III, c. 46 (Local and Personal).

Bath trust.[49] In 1873 the trust was dissolved, and subsequently the area was administered by the Sodbury Highway Board.[50]

In 1749 a band of colliers 'cut down the Pike at Yeat, and also the large Elm that had stood there for 100 Years.'[51] Reports concerning the incident do not confirm whether the colliers were from Yate, as it formed part of a broader phase of turnpike breaking affecting the Bristol region in July and August that year. Protests against turnpiking had begun in the area from *c*.1727, and a similar disturbance may have occurred in Yate in 1731.[52] Nonetheless, the gate remained operational.[53] Known as 'Yate Elm Pike' its precise location is uncertain,[54] but it probably stood in Station Road near its junction with Church Lane.[55] When the turnpike trust expired the tollhouse and garden were sold to Jonathan Corbett Neale, who owned the White Lion inn and adjacent properties.[56] Although the building was demolished, an area next to the inn was named Turnpike Close.[57] A second gate stood further east, at the junction of Love Lane with the Sodbury to Wickwar road.[58]

Railways

Before 1800 Bristol's demand for coal prompted attempts to establish alternative distributive networks from the pits north of the city. These included in 1793 a proposed canal to link the Avon at Bristol with the Thames and Severn canal near Cirencester, via Stapleton, Coalpit Heath, Yate and Sodbury. Neither this nor any other canal scheme was executed, being overtaken by the railway.[59]

By an act of 1828 the Bristol and Gloucestershire Railway was empowered to build a line from St Philip's in Bristol to Coalpit Heath for the carriage of stone and coal.[60] In 1835 the line was opened,[61] and I.K. Brunel was appointed in 1839 as the engineer to extend the line to Gloucester.[62] The section through Yate was the first part of this extension, and was built between 1841 and 1844. The line entered the parish from Westerleigh at the western limit of Station Road, extended north to follow the eastern edge of Engine Common, and then crossed Yate Lower Common, remaining close to the collieries; it then turned east, and left the parish north of Hall End via the Wickwar

49 Union of Turnpike Trusts Act, 12–13 Vic. c. 46.
50 GA, Q/AH/23; ibid. HB 15; for 20th-century roads, below p. 23.
51 *Glouc. J.* 8 Aug. 1749.
52 R.W. Malcolmson, '"A set of ungovernable people": the Kingswood colliers in the eighteenth century' in J. Brewer and J. Styles (eds.) *An Ungovernable People* (1980), 100, 110; A. Randall and A. Charlesworth (eds.), *Markets, Market Culture and Popular Protest in Eighteenth-Century Britain and Ireland* (1996), 46–68.
53 *Glouc. J.* Nov. 1778.
54 P.A. Couzens, *Annals of a Parish viz Yate* (1990), 49.
55 GDR, T 1/207.
56 GA, Q/RD/2/18–40; Q/RI/164; GDR, T 1/207; *Census,* 1891.
57 Site visit, Sept. 2012.
58 GA, Q/RI/164; HER S. Glos. no. 2088; Cossons, *Ind. Arch. of the Bristol Region*, 255.
59 GA, Q/RUm/3; C.G. Maggs, *The Bristol and Glouc. Railway and the Avon and Glos. Railway* (1992), 5.
60 Bristol & Glouc. Railway Act, 9 Geo. IV, c. 93 (Local and Personal); GA, D 6822/101.
61 *Bristol Mercury*, 8 Aug. 1835; Maggs, *Bristol and Glouc. Railway*, 7.
62 *Railway Times*, 1839; Bristol & Glouc. Railway Act, 2–3 Vic. c. 56 (Local and Personal); Maggs, *Bristol and Glouc. Railway,* 11–13.

Figure 2 *Station staff and travellers about to board a passenger train at Yate Station, c.1910.*

Tunnel. A road bridge over the line was built at Hall End Lane in 1843, and a station and goods shed, both of brick, south of Yate Junction in 1844. The line opened throughout on 6 July 1844.[63]

The renamed Bristol and Gloucester Railway formed a significant link between Bristol and Birmingham, and thus between northern and midland cities and the south-west, and via the Great Western Railway with London.[64] Through travel was complicated, however, by the change from broad gauge between Bristol and Gloucester to narrow (or standard) gauge between Gloucester and Birmingham. In 1848, after the line became part of the Midland Railway,[65] legislation allowed the company to establish a standard gauge line from Gloucester to Stonehouse, and mixed gauge on through Yate to Bristol.[66] In 1872 all lines in the Gloucester district were converted to standard gauge.[67]

The arrival of the railway brought Yate an important distributive network for its stone and coal, and stimulated passenger travel and subsidiary amenities in the area.[68] Yate Junction became a regional hub. A branch line to Thornbury was constructed between 1869 and 1872,[69] and by 1908 the Westerleigh loop, just south of Yate Junction, connected the Midland Railway, via a branch line from the station, to the Great Western's South Wales

63   GA, Q/RUm/156; Q/RI/164; NHL, no. 1234324, The goods shed, Yate railway station: 12 Feb. 2015; *Bristol Mercury*, 1 Apr. 1843, 31 March 1844, 13 July 1844.

64   *Railway Times*, 1841, 404; Maggs, *Bristol and Glouc. Railway,* 15.

65   GA, D 6822/101; Maggs, *Bristol and Glouc. Railway,* 25–7.

66   Midland Railway Act, 11 and 12 Vic. c. 131 (Local and Personal); Maggs, *Bristol and Glouc. Railway,* 30.

67   Maggs, *Bristol and Glouc. Railway,* 31.

68   See pp. 47–50, 53–4.

69   *Bristol Mercury*, Sept. 1869 and Sept. 1872; OS Maps 6", Glos. LXIX.NW (1886 edn).

and Bristol Direct Line.[70] Industrial lines from quarries and collieries in the parish were also built to connect to the Midland Railway. From *c*.1847 a tramway linked Bury Hill quarry (east of Yate Court) to limekilns adjacent to the main railway line. It was still in use in 1903, but abandoned by *c*.1924.[71] By 1886 another tramway existed between Yate Collieries Nos. 1 and 2 on Engine Common, and Colliery 1 was linked directly to the main line by a branch, closed in 1890.[72] The Thornbury to Yate branch line was closed to passengers in 1944, and to general goods traffic in 1967. The line remained open as far as Tytherington to serve a limestone quarry which closed in 2013, the remainder of the branch line being designated as 'Out of use (temporary)' in September of that year.[73]

Passenger trains no longer called at Yate after January 1965,[74] but as the new town developed and commuter traffic caused road congestion, a popular campaign to restore a service was mounted.[75] In May 1989 a new station funded by Avon County Council and British Rail was opened, offering a regular rail service between Yate, Lawrence Hill and Bristol Temple Meads, with a feeder bus operating from Chipping Sodbury and North Yate.[76] In 2014 rail passenger services ran from Bristol via Yate to Cheltenham, Gloucester and beyond.[77]

Buses

Although there was no service for the parish, the horse omnibus of J.H. Bees delivered passengers from Chipping Sodbury to meet every train at Yate station in 1897, and Jones and Son also provided a daily service from Chipping Sodbury to Bristol.[78] By 1935 the Bristol Tramways and Carriage Co. ran motor omnibuses on the same route, and to Bath, 'at frequent intervals'.[79] From the 1950s, Yate's manufactories provided a regular bus service for its employees living outside the parish.[80] With the development of the new town, regular bus services were established. In *c*.1965 buses from Bristol stopped along Station Road en route to Chipping Sodbury, Swindon, Stroud and Cirencester, in addition to other 'country services' also from Bristol.[81] In 2012 eight operators provided buses in the Yate and Sodbury area to Bristol, Bath and other South Gloucestershire settlements.[82]

Settlement

Early History

There is modest evidence for pre-Roman activity within the ancient parish. Isolated examples of Neolithic, Early Bronze Age and Iron Age tools have been found across the

70   OS Maps 6", Glos. LXIX.SW (1903, 1924 edns); Maggs, *Bristol and Glouc. Railway*, 35.
71   OS Maps 6", Glos. LXIX.NW (1903, 1924 edns); HER S. Glos. no. 2064.
72   OS Map 6", Glos. LXIX.NW (1886 edn); see pp. 48–9.
73   Buchanan and Cossons, *Ind. Arch. of Bristol Region*, 294, 297; Network Rail, STNC/G1/2013/WEST/565, http://www.networkrail.co.uk/searchresult.aspx?q=tytherington (accessed 11 Feb. 2015).
74   YHC, D/1003/A Public Notice, 1964–5.
75   YHC, *Sodbury and Yate Gazette*, 3 July 1987.
76   Ibid. 19 May 1989; GA, D 6822/101.
77   Local inf.
78   *Kelly's Dir. Glos.* (1897 edn), 107.
79   *Kelly's Dir. Glos.* (1935 edn), 112.
80   See *Social History*, p. 70.
81   YHC, D/310 Shopping Centre Brochure (*c*.1965).
82   South Glos. Council, *Yate Travel Guide* (*c*.2012, accessed 2015).

parish, often as a result of quarrying.[83] A Bronze Age burnt mound with associated water troughs, post holes and wooden structure, were found at Peg Hill, between Goose Green and the Sodbury to Wickwar Road.[84] Earthworks indicative of early settlement and land cultivation have been identified in areas that later became manorial seats, at Brinsham and close to Yate Court.[85]

Archaeological evidence of a significant Roman settlement or small town has been found at Hall End Farm, extending into the parish from the north. It covered 16 ha. next to the Ladden Brook WNW of Hall End Farm, and 2 km south of Wickwar.[86] The settlement straddled a metalled road up to 11 m. wide, which ran from Bitton towards Gloucester across Engine Common, extending north through the fields of Great and Little Blacklands in Yate.[87] Occupied between the 2nd and 4th centuries, the town may have been built on the site of an earlier fort, to which a distinctive ditch along its north-eastern edge belonged.[88] It consisted of simple stone cottages and higher-status aisled houses, adorned with decorative masonry.[89] Evidence of commercial activity has been found, including debris from a smithy or iron furnace,[90] and less extensive finds of pottery, and the presence of a platform, have been discovered further south near Yate Court.[91]

The Hall End settlement has been identified with *Milidunum*, a town recorded in the post-Roman *Ravenna Cosmography*,[92] although this identification remains uncertain.[93] The settlement may have survived to serve as a garrisoned outpost during the 6th century, forming part of a defensive triangle including *Abona* (Sea Mills) and Bath.[94]

Saxon Origins

References to Yate in Saxon charters offer little evidence about its extent. A lost charter of *c*.716 detailed a gift of lands at 'Gete' from Ethelbald, king of the Mercians, to Eanulf.[95] This gift is recited in a charter of *c*.779, whereby the Mercian king Offa and Ealdred, sub-king of the Hwicce, granted 10 *mansiones* (hides) at Yate to St Mary's church, Worcester.[96] Its authenticity is doubtful, since sections have been copied from other extant charters,[97] and the reference to St Mary's, Worcester, a 10th-century foundation, is anachronistic;[98]

83 HER S. Glos. nos 2063, 2089, 2090, 12982.

84 *Trans. BGAS*, 132 (2014) 273.

85 HER S. Glos. no. 2892, 3063, 5272, 5273, 19716, identified from aerial photographs, and site investigations *c*.1979 conducted by R. Iles.

86 *English Heritage*, Scheduled Monument no. 1021404.

87 Ibid.; I. Margary, *Roman Roads in Britain* (1973 edn), 141; *Trans. BGAS*, 121 (2003) 287; GDR, T 1/207.

88 *English Heritage*, Scheduled Monument no. 1021404.

89 *Trans. BGAS*, 121 (2003), 287.

90 *English Heritage*, Scheduled Monument no. 1021404.

91 HER S. Glos. Parish Survey, 2061 (1978); R. Iles, 'Archaeology in Avon', *Avon Past* (1979), 33.

92 D. Higgins, *History of the Bristol Region in the Roman Period* (Bristol Branch of the Historical Association, pamphlet 115, 2005), 11.

93 A.L.F. Rivet, *Place Names of Roman Britain* (1979), 190, 200, 206.

94 Higgins, *History of the Bristol Region in the Sub-Roman and Early Anglo-Saxon Periods* (Bristol Branch of the Historical Association, pamphlet 118, 2006), 10, 17.

95 H.P.R. Finberg, *Early Charters of the West Midlands* (1961), 34–5 (no. 18).

96 P.H. Sawyer, *Anglo-Saxon charters* (1968), 108–9 (no. 147); Finberg, *Early Charters*, 39–40 (no. 37).

97 Sawyer, *Anglo-Saxon Charters*, 108–9.

98 *VCH Worcs*. II, 94–5.

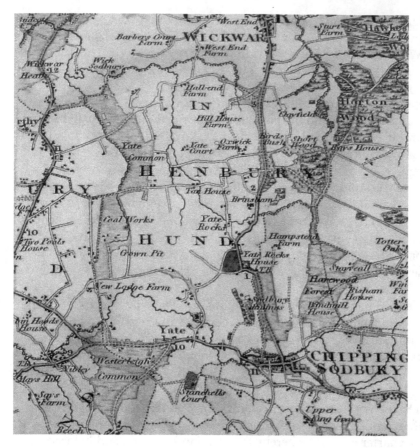

Map 3 *Detail from Greenwood's Map of Gloucestershire, 1824.*

but despite substitutions and interpolations, charters of this nature may embody the substance of a genuine original.[99]

A second charter of *c*.716, confirmed *c*.793, granted estates at Westbury-on-Trym and Henbury to Worcester in terms similar to those of Yate.[100] Since this grant may have marked the foundation of a monastic settlement at Westbury,[101] it is possible that a minster was established at Yate at the same time,[102] but no physical or documentary evidence has been found to confirm this.[103] These 8th-century charters may nevertheless relate to the acquisition of estates, including Westbury, Henbury, Redwick, Stoke Bishop and Yate, by the bishops of Worcester, their owner in 1066.[104]

The Yate charters do not define the Saxon estate's boundaries, but some indication of its southern limit may be deduced from a survey of 950.[105] This describes the north-eastern extent of Westerleigh (abutting Yate): from *Stanford*, crossing the Frome, to the

99   Finberg, *Early Charters*, 39–40 (no. 37).
100   Ibid. 38 (no. 17), 42 (no. 50).
101   *VCH Glos.* II, 106.
102   P.A. Couzens, *Annals of a Parish viz Yate* (1990), 6.
103   C. Heighway, *Anglo-Saxon Glos.* (1987), Appendix 1, 167.
104   *Domesday*, 452.
105   Finberg, *Early Charters*, 54 (no. 100).

'stone bank' and from the latter to the 'gate of the deer-leap', thence to the 'enclosures' and on to the 'king's ride'. *Stanford* or the 'stone ford' has been located where the road north from Yate Station crosses the River Frome; and Stover, immediately west of the railway station, may be a corruption of *Stan Ofer*, or 'stone bank'. The 'deer-leap' landmark implies the edge of inclosed woodland, and the 'kings ride' a way through the wood.[106] Indeed in this context the name Yate (*geat* in Old English) most probably signifies a gate or entrance into the wood.[107]

It is uncertain whether later parish boundaries reflects those of the Saxon estates, because the land holdings of forest settlements tended to fluctuate as they attempted to extend cultivation into previously forested areas.[108] For Yate this uncertainty may be significant as the early medieval parish fell entirely within Horwood forest and consequently its extent may have changed over time.

Further evidence of pre-Conquest settlement in the Yate area may also be found in a grant of 990 by Oswald, bishop of Worcester. A postscript refers to the *worthig* (inclosure or farmstead) at *Brynnes hamme*, which may be equated with Brinsham in the east of the ancient parish, where archaeological evidence of prehistoric and mediaeval settlement has been found.[109]

Population

As Yate was assessed jointly with the bishop of Worcester's other holdings in Brentry hundred in 1086, and with Itchington in 1327, no separate estimates of early population can be made.[110] A 1522 muster roll included 62 men of Yate, and *c*.65 taxpayers were listed between 1522 and 1527.[111] In 1551, 240 communicants were recorded.[112] During the following century Yate's population appears relatively stable, with 83 able-bodied men included in the military survey of 1608, 70 households assessed for the hearth tax in 1662, and 86 in 1664 and 1672.[113] In 1603 there were 195 communicants, and 257 in 1676.[114] Total population probably increased after 1700, from estimates of 320 in *c*.1710–35 to 412 by *c*.1779.[115]

106   G.B. Grundy, *Saxon Charters and Field Names of Glos.* (1935), 211–18.
107   *PN Glos.* III, 44.
108   Grundy, *Saxon Charters*, 217.
109   Finberg, *Early Charters*, 63 (no. 136); *PN Glos.* III, 44; see pp. 31–4.
110   *Domesday* 452 (lists 91 villeins, bordars, slaves and coliberts in Henbury, Redwick, Stoke Bishop and Yate); P. Franklin, *Taxpayers of Medieval Glos* (1993), 89 (lists 44 taxpayers for both parishes).
111   *Military Surv. of Glos, 1522*, 42–3; *Bristol and Glos. Lay Subsidy, 1523–27*, 132–4, 301–2.
112   J. Gairdner, 'Bishop Hooper's Visitation of Gloucester', *EHR* 19 (1904), 116.
113   Smith, *Men and Armour*, 215–17; TNA, E 179/116/554 (1662), E 179/247/16 (1664, includes 20 exemptions), E 179/247/13 (1672, includes 18 exemptions).
114   *Compton Census*, 536.
115   Atkyns, *Glos.* I, 857; *Benson's Surv.* 39, Rudder, *Glos.* 855.

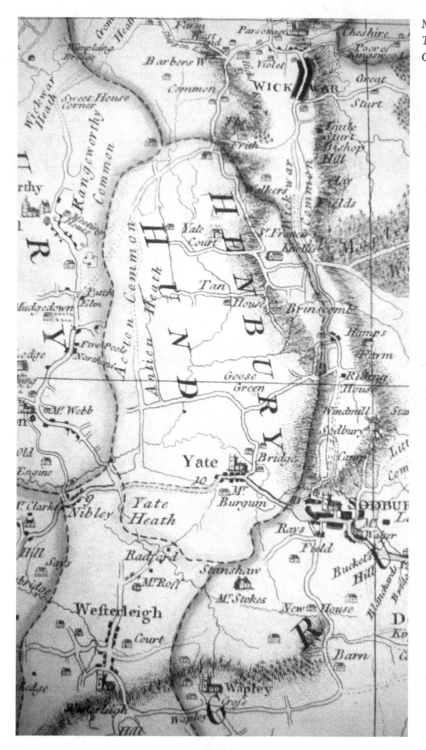

Map 4 *Detail from Taylor's Map of Gloucestershire, 1777.*

Table 1 *Population 1801–1981*

Census Year	Population	Census Year	Population
1801	654	1901	1,279
1811	717	1911	1,309
1821	827	1921	1,332
1831	824	1931	1,559
1841	1,057	1951	2,321
1851	1,080	1961	3,898
1881	1,255	1971	10,182
1891	1,190	1981	13,599

By 1801 the total had reached 654, nearly doubling to 1,279 by 1901. Growth during the century was steady, although a marked increase between 1831 and 1841 reflected the introduction of the railway, and there was a small decline between 1881 and 1891.[116] The arrival of manufacturing and light industry after 1920 presaged another significant rise, from 1,332 in 1921 to 1,559 in 1931. The wartime influx and continued expansion of industry in the 1940s accounted for further increases into the 1950s.[117] With urban development the population more than doubled, exceeding 10,000 in 1971. Growth continued, although at a steadier pace into the 1980s. The population of the parish (as redrawn in 1988) in 2001 was 21,789, and 21,603 in 2011.[118]

Built Character

Medieval to c.1900

Medieval settlement within the parish was concentrated around St Mary's church, forming the core of the village, with more diffuse hamlets in the north and very south of the parish, focused on the manorial centres. Archaeological evidence suggests that pre-Roman and Roman occupation favoured the same locations as the medieval and early modern communities.[119] Subsequent development up to *c.*1900 largely followed the main road (Station Road) running east–west through the parish, and after 1840 the railway stimulated concerted commercial and residential expansion in its south-western quarter.[120]

St Mary's church stands just north of the former turnpike road, bounded to the east by Church Lane, which leads northwards to Goose Green common, where it splits into Broad Lane, westward towards Iron Acton, and Peg Hill, eastward in the direction of the ridge.[121] The 12th-century church was substantially rebuilt after 1485, and its tower has been lauded as a splendid example of Perpendicular architecture in the region. Built

---

116 *Census*, 1801–81.
117 *Census*, 1911–61; G.E. Payne, *Survey of Glos.* (1947), 305.
118 *Census*, 1971–2011 (1971 = 10,182, 1981 = 13,599).
119 See pp. 10–13.
120 OS Maps 1", sheet 35 (1830 edn); 6", Glos. LXIX.NW, SW (1886 edn); GDR, T 1/207.
121 OS Maps 6", Glos. LXIV.SW, LXIX.NW, SW (1886 edn), 25", Glos. LXIX.6 (1882 edn).

Figure 3 *View of Goose Green Farm, a 17th-century farmhouse, c.1910.*

of Pennant sandstone the church stood at the core of the village and provided a locus of medieval settlement away from the manorial estates.[122] North of the church towards Goose Green and north of Broad Lane lay open fields bounded by the river Frome.[123] A parish poorhouse and the premises that later became the White Lion inn,[124] both situated on Church Road, were among the non-agricultural buildings that clustered around the church from the 16th century.[125]

Goose Green features prominently on maps from 1777, but may have been a much older settlement. Church Lane, Broad Lane and Peg Hill all converged on the common at the centre of the 'Church End' of the parish, and by the 18th century small dwellings clustered on the periphery of this green.[126] Other commons within the parish were also important resources for Yate's poorer inhabitants. Yate Lower Common on the western edge of the parish accommodated smaller, informal settlements from the medieval period through to the 19th century.[127]

Away from the village core, the manorial demesne lands constituted the centres of medieval communities. The grandest of these, Yate Court, stood north of Tanhouse Lane, and was a 13th-century moated and crenellated manor house whose estate included a walled deer park, corn mill and millpond, and rabbit warren. Rebuilt by Maurice, Lord Berkeley during the 16th century, this mansion was destroyed during the Civil Wars,

122 OS Map 25", Glos. LXIX.6 (1882 edn); Verey and Brooks, *Glos.* II, 55, 824; site visit Sept. 2012; see pp. 89–90.
123 OS Map 25", Glos. LXIX.6 (1882 edn); GDR, T 1/207; Q/RI/164.
124 OS Map 25", Glos. LXIX.6 (1882 edn); NHL, no. 1321156, The White Lion: 12 Feb. 2015.
125 GA, Q/RI/164; GDR wills 1576/36.
126 Taylor, *Map of Glos.* (1777); OS Map 25", Glos. LXIX.6 (1882 edn); GDR, T 1/207; Q/RI/164.
127 Rudder, *Glos.* 855; HER S. Glos. no. 14419; GDR, T 1/207.

*c.*1644, but its ruins survived.[128] Its deer park covered *c.*350 a. with a circumference of *c.*2½ miles, and around its perimeter, particularly to the north, and along Tanhouse Lane in the south, there is evidence of medieval cultivation.[129] Ridge and furrow at Stanshawes in the south, and Brinsham in the east, indicate former arable fields which were probably worked from settlements nearby.[130] Brinsham manor also encompassed the hamlet of Yate Rocks, straddling a tributary of the Ladden Brook.[131]

Early modern development largely followed the pattern of the medieval settlements. Although little Tudor building survives, Yate boasted fine examples of 17th-century gabled farmhouses of Pennant stone characteristic of the region. Several occupy previously developed sites, and appear to be extensively modified earlier structures.[132]

Frith Farm, standing near the northern edge of the parish, is the largest of the early modern farmhouses. Laid out on an L-plan, the house is of two storeys with cellar, dairy and bakehouse, and attics in three stone gables. Thick walls at the west end of the building and re-used roof timbers suggest a 16th-century origin, although alterations were made in the 17th and 18th centuries. The stonework and mortar structure was protected by roughcast, partially decorated with a pattern of a rose and four fleurs-de-lis within a lozenge shape. Other decorative features were found in the moulded doorcases and carved staircase, more typical of wealthier 17th-century properties.[133]

Hall End Farm, formerly known as Baynhams, overlies Roman archaeology in north Yate and, like Frith Farm, consists of a pre-17th-century core which underwent significant alterations by 1700, to create a substantial gentleman's house. Built in a three-room and through-passage layout, an unheated parlour at the northern end suggests a 16th-century origin. The length of the foundations (*c.*30 m) suggests that a medieval longhouse may have occupied the site. Before 1700 its owner, Richard Hill, created a formal garden including bee boles and fishponds.[134]

Less opulent 17th- and 18th-century farmhouses were also to be found along Tanhouse Lane and in Yate village.[135] Goose Green Farm, north of the common, was centred on a modest 17th-century L-plan farmhouse, of coursed rubble, with two gables and mullioned windows.[136] It too was probably remodelled on an earlier building; the

128 OS Map 6", Glos. LXIV.SW (1886 edn); GDR, T 1/207; M. Salter, *Castles of Glos. and Bristol* (2002), 39; Verey and Brooks, *Glos.* II, 830; see p. 29.
129 S. Lay and R. Iles, 'Medieval Deer Parks in Avon', *Avon Past,* 1 (1979), 9–10; GDR, T 1/207..
130 HER S. Glos. nos. 17548 and 18973.
131 GDR, T 1/207; see *Manors and Estates.*
132 OS Maps 1", sheet 35 (1830 edn); 6", Glos. LXIV.SW, LXIX.NW, SW (1886 edn); GDR, T 1/207; GA, Q/RI/164 I; L.J. Hall, *Rural Houses of North Avon and South Glos. 1400–1720* (1983), 30–2.
133 NHL, no. 1128768, Frith Farm and Bakehouse at SE, Frith Lane, Wickwar: 12 Feb. 2015; Hall, *Rural Houses* 297–9; Verey and Brooks, *Glos.* II, 830.
134 HER S. Glos. no. 4384; GA, D 1610/E120 1659; Site visit Oct. 2012; M. Isaac, *Farms of Yate* (*c.*2004), 10; Hall, *Rural Houses*, 12–13, 306.
135 OS Maps 6", Glos. LXIV.SW, LXIX.NW; NHL, nos. 1128750, Goose Green Farmhouse; 1128751, Lattimore farmhouse and attached barn and shelter sheds and service wing: 12 Feb 2015; Hall, *Rural Houses,* 21; Verey and Brooks, *Glos.* II, p. 89.
136 OS Map 25", Glos. LXIX.6 (1882 edn); NHL, no. 1128750; Hall, *Rural Houses,* 303; Verey and Brooks, *Glos.* II, 87, 829.

stairs with solid oak treads, the window mullions, and remnants of a rare mock-panelled painted wall were consistent with 16th-century properties in neighbouring parishes.[137]

Grander building projects were undertaken after 1700, including creating and replacing manorial seats. In c.1722 Robert Oxwick of London, then lord of Yate manor, built Oxwick Hall east of the dilapidated remains of Yate Court.[138] Described as 'a curious and unsophisticated blend of gabled vernacular and provincial Baroque', the three-storey house, of Pennant stone with brick dressings, has five unequal gables symmetrically arranged either side of a recessed central bay.[139]

The manorial seat was removed again before 1800 to Yate House, a two-storey, neo-classical influenced country house of ashlar masonry. It stood in the east of the parish, south of Yate Rocks, and had an adjacent lodge and extensive gardens.[140] Ridge House, constructed somewhat later, and Chipping Sodbury union workhouse of c.1835, both near the ridge and Yate House, also reflected the availability of limestone rather than the more usual Pennant sandstone. The workhouse, designed by Scott and Moffatt, employed a Tudor style intended to create an attractive and humane structure.[141]

Improved roads through Yate in the 18th century and the railway's arrival after 1840 encouraged residential and commercial ribbon development.[142] From an estimated 80 dwellings in the parish in 1712,[143] the number had more than doubled by 1831 to 174; and by 1931 it had doubled again, to 371.[144] While much new building was focused along Station Road, the collieries also generated a distinct community further north, running the length of Engine Common. In addition to miners' cottages, a school, public house and Baptist chapel were established there before 1900.[145]

The Victorian building boom included significant individual houses in the south of the parish, and at the village core. In 1874 Robert Nathaniel Hooper rebuilt Stanshawes Court as an impressive Gothic mansion, and a noted church architect, William Douglas Caröe,[146] rebuilt Poole Court in c.1850. This 'stately home', brick-built with ashlar dressings, was set back from Station Road, close to the church, and renovated a century later as a new office and civic centre for Yate town council. Caröe also renovated St Mary's church between 1897 and 1900; the adjacent school was rebuilt before 1900.[147]

The 'New Town' Development, c.1900–c.1988

In 1900 Yate was still essentially rural. Residential and commercial development was concentrated along Station Road, close to the old village centre around the church, and

---

137 Hall, *Rural Houses*, 303.

138 See pp.29–30.

139 Verey and Brooks, *Glos*. II, 830.

140 OS Maps 1", sheet 35 (1830 edn); 6", Glos. LXIX.NW (1886 edn).

141 NHL, no. 1128772, Ridgewood, Yate offices of Avon county social services: 12 Feb 2012; HER S. Glos. no 13607; Verey and Brooks, *Glos*. II, 116, 828; see p. 76.

142 OS Maps 25", Glos. LXIX.9, 10 (1882 edn); OS *Reference Book* 1869–70; see for example, HER S. Glos. no 19666; Verey and Brooks, *Glos*. II, 824.

143 Rudder, *Glos*. 855.

144 *Census* 1831–1931.

145 OS Maps 25", Glos. LXIX.1, 5 (1881 edn).

146 *ODNB*, s.a. Caröe, William Douglas (1857–1938) (accessed 12 Feb. 2015).

147 OS Map 25", Glos. LXIX.6 (1882 edn), 6", LXIX.NW (1924 edn); Verey and Brooks, *Glos*. II, 828–9; see pp. 100–2.

clustered around the railway station further west. Much of the north of the parish was farmland, with small outlying settlements persisting at Yate Rocks and along Tanhouse Lane.[148] Industrial development after 1920, triggered by wartime military aviation and the ongoing extractive industries, transformed Yate gradually from railway village to new town. The industrial focus lay to the north of Station Road, between Yate Junction and the Frome, where in 1916 the Royal Flying Corps established an airfield. The site was developed as an aircraft test and repair depot, and Poole Court was commandeered as the officers' mess. Military use ended in 1918, and the area was subsequently used to manufacture aircraft, electric motors and domestic appliances.[149]

The population had already increased by 42 per cent between 1931 and 1939; wartime production between 1939 and 1945, and industrial expansion in its aftermath stimulated a further influx of people into the parish, creating a greater demand for housing.[150] Limited development had taken place in the east of the parish by c.1954. The Ridge estate included Firgrove Crescent, semi-detached houses arranged in a 'spider's web' and linked by a route descending towards Station Road; and two terraces of similarly arranged houses at the Ridgeway, just above the main thoroughfare. The Crescent was designed around a circular green, and had a primary school on its periphery.[151] In addition a street and two closes of semi-detached houses were built in the west of the parish, over Eggshill Common.[152]

In 1952 Bristol Corporation, Sodbury Rural District Council and Gloucestershire County Council agreed to expand Yate as part of an 'overspill scheme' to manage the expansion of Bristol's urban population. The scheme also included the development of Warmley, Keynsham and other settlements ringing Bristol. The District Council purchased the former airfield site, and in 1954 made plans to build 800 housing units on an area of 100 a., including bungalows and blocks of flats.[153] In the long-term, 3,000 new homes were planned for the Yate–Sodbury area. [154]

The 'new town' plan for Yate was not outlined fully until 1959,[155] and did not follow the development model set out in the 1946 New Towns Act. Expansion was not administered centrally, but was a cooperative effort between the local councils and private developers, empowered by the 1952 Town Development Act.[156] Although it was not, therefore, one of the statutory new towns, the rationale underpinning them applied also to Yate.[157]

In order to avoid the social, economic and environmental degeneration equated with 'urban sprawl', Bristol's growth was corralled by the green belt encompassing the city. Yate, although accommodating Bristol overspill, was not to become a dormitory

---

148 OS Maps 6", Glos. LXIV.SW, LXIX.NW, SW (1903 edn).
149 OS Maps 25", Glos. LXIX. 5, 6, 9 (1921 edn); HER S. Glos. no 8899; Walker, *Bristol Region*, 326; see pp. 54–6.
150 Payne, *Survey of Glos*, 305.
151 OS Maps 25", ST 7182, 7282 (1955 edns); *Bristol Evening Post*, 13 Aug. 1954.
152 OS Map 25", ST 7082 (1955 edn).
153 GA, DA 33/132/1/10–11.
154 *Bristol Evening Post*, 13 Aug. 1954; GA, DA 33/132/1/11.
155 *Bristol Evening Post*, 22 Aug. 1958; YHC, D/299.
156 YHC, D/299; Sir. H. Wells, 'Agencies and Finance', in H. Evans, *New Towns: The British Experience* (Town and Country Planning Association, 1972), 31–3.
157 H. Evans, Introduction to *New Towns: The British Experience*, 6–9.

suburb.[158] The Yate–Sodbury area was selected as appropriate for development as it already constituted the nucleus of a town. It had its own industry and resources suitable for supplying the development, a road network, and an existing social structure that it was hoped would provide the basis for a new and homogeneous community not solely dependent on Bristol for employment.[159] Limited new construction was planned around Chipping Sodbury, but both popular and local political opinions favoured the preservation of the town's historic architecture over expansion. Yate was, therefore, the site for the majority of the new building.[160]

Residential Development

Five neighbourhoods were proposed. The airfield or 'Yate' development and the Ridge estate would be completed and expanded; further housing was planned for Westerleigh Common, and for the Stanshawes estate, south of Station Road, focused around the former manorial seat; and limited development was outlined north and south of Chipping Sodbury High Street. Each neighbourhood would have a shopping centre, schools and recreational open spaces. In addition to these 'sub-centres', a new town centre would be laid out east of St Mary's church, on the north side of Station Road, to provide a shopping centre and civic amenities.[161]

Private developers had bought much of the land proposed for the new town, and to check and control development the local authorities established a formal plan for urban expansion in 1959.[162] This was superseded by another in 1966, with further amendments in 1967 and 1970. Significant alterations were made subsequently during the development process.[163]

The building of the largest estate, at Stanshawes, was delayed in 1964 when the incoming council planning officer rejected the plans submitted by the contractors, Stanshawes Estate Ltd., for the fourth phase of the development. The planners had provisionally agreed to 1,119 houses and a block of flats on an 88 a. site, reflecting the perceived need for smaller housing units for single men and women moving to Yate from Bristol.[164] The new planning officer expressed concern that the building plans submitted, particularly the predominance of uniform terraces, would result in an economically and socially unvaried environment. He proposed an alternative Radburn-style layout, which emphasised the segregation of pedestrians and traffic, encouraging a variety of dwellings and the use of green spaces as part of the pedestrian network. His proposals were supported by the local residents' association, and incorporated into the 1966 planning document. By August 1967 the fourth phase of the Stanshawes estate, adhering to the new models proposed by the planning office, was largely complete. The Radburn-style

158 YHC, D/299/A; *Bristol Evening Post*, 13 Aug. 1954.
159 YHC, D/299/A.
160 *Bristol Evening Post,* 22 Aug. 1958.
161 YHC, D/299/A (1959).
162 YHC, D/299/A; *Bristol Evening Post*, 13 Aug. 1954; YHC, D/299/A (1959); GA, DA 33/701/3/4; DA 33/132/1/11.
163 YHC, D/294; YHC, D/296; GA, DA 33/701/3/4; DA 33/132/1/11.
164 This para, YHC, D/287/1–2, *Sodbury and Yate Gazette*, 1 Feb. 1964 and 4 Apr. 1964; *Bristol Evening Post,* 22 Aug. 1958; GA, DC/89/1/5; GA, D A 33/132/1/11; Verey and Brooks, *Glos.* II, 829.

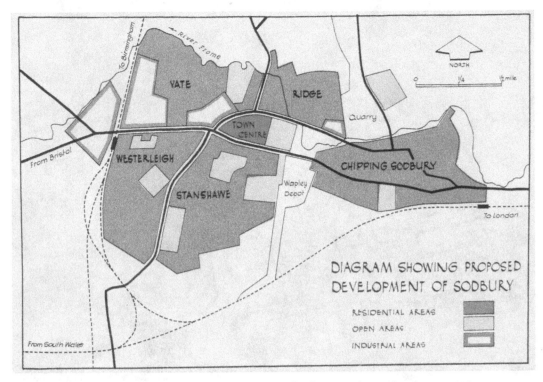

Figure 4 *The five estates planned for the Yate new town development, from a brochure c.1959.*

arrangement was continued throughout the development south of Station Road into the 1970s.

Plans to develop Westerleigh Common were abandoned when, in *c.*1962, Westerleigh parish council bought the land in order to preserve its status as a public open space.[165] Further attempts to develop part of the common were defeated by a popular campaign in 1988.[166] Development north of Station Road was limited during the 1960s and 1970s by celestine extraction, since the new town plan stipulated that areas where the mineral could be won and worked would not be built on until all deposits were exhausted.[167]

Between 1951 and 1961 the number of houses within the parish almost doubled, from 612 to 1,125. The number of households in 1971 was 3,067, and 4,637 in 1981.[168] By the 1980s development had begun north of the river Frome to Goose Green Way, including detached and semi-detached houses, laid out to follow existing street lines. Further development north of Goose Green Way was undertaken during the 1990s.[169] In 2012 South Gloucestershire council held consultations for further development north of the existing urban area.[170]

---

165 YHC, D/294 (1968); G. Tily, 'Yate's Open Spaces', in Couzens, *Annals of a Parish*, 52–5.
166 GA, D 6822/70; see p. 66.
167 GA, DC /89/1/5; YHC, D/294 (1968).
168 *Census*, 1951–81.
169 OS Map, 1:10,000 sheet ST 78SW (1989 edn); Verey and Brooks, *Glos.* II, 829.
170 South Glos. Council, 'Issues and Options Consultation: Urban Expansion at Yate/Chipping Sodbury' (accessed 2012).

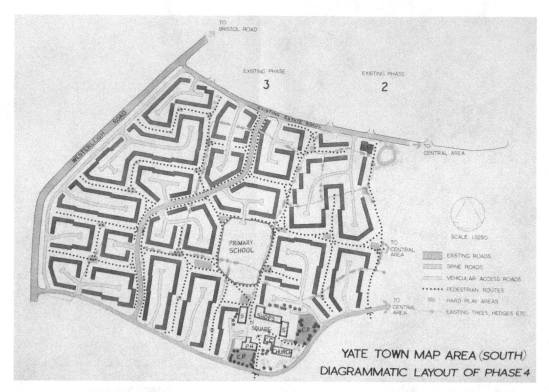

Figure 5 *Original diagram of the Radburn-style layout adopted in the south Yate housing development, c.1964.*

Commercial Development and Distributive Networks

In 1964 industry was concentrated in three areas: along Station Road; to the west on the former airfield site; and to the east just outside Chipping Sodbury.[171] Although the planning authorities encouraged industries to continue and grow, so as to sustain employment within the emerging town, they also sought to control its location. Land in the parish, west of the railway line at Stover, was allotted for expansion, and to relocate 'non-conforming' industrial and commercial enterprises away from Station Road and the new town centre.[172]

The shopping centre provided for in the 1959 town plan was opened in September 1965.[173] The precinct, to a cruciform design with clean, angular lines and mixed material construction, was intended to reflect the progressive nature of Yate's development. More akin to an American shopping mall, it was the only commercial centre of its kind in the region, outside Bristol, until the 1970s or later.[174] Within the central square a statue by Franta Belsky, entitled 'Four Seasons', provided a focal point; the abstract piece stood 17 ft. tall and incorporated a fountain. The statue itself deteriorated and was removed

171 GA, DC/89/1/5.
172 YHC, D/296 (1967); YHC, D/296; see *Economic History*.
173 YHC, *Sodbury and Yate Gazette*, 25 Sep 1965.
174 Pers. comm. YHC; Verey and Brooks, *Glos.* II, 827; Walker, *Bristol Region*, 331.

when the centre was renovated in 1990, but the refurbished complex was renamed Four Seasons.[175] Civic amenities were accommodated within and adjacent to the shopping centre, including a public library, and sports and leisure centre.[176] Other smaller shopping and amenity 'sub-centres' were gradually established within the new estates.[177]

Developing an adequate road network to serve the new town proved a long-running source of frustration. The 1966 plan and 1967 town map outlined the local authorities' key concerns. Station Road remained the primary distribution route through the parish, so that increasing levels of traffic and congestion in the town centre became a problem; but a by-pass to link Yate with the M4 and M5 motorways was deemed prohibitively expensive.[178] The Radburn model sought to reduce traffic through the areas where vehicular and pedestrian routes were segregated. A system of primary and secondary distributor roads had therefore been planned to circulate traffic around the residential development and feed local traffic into the culs-de-sac. The intention was to implement this in stages as building progressed.[179]

In 1978 the newly constituted town council raised a public complaint regarding the perceived 'neglect' of the road network in Yate. They cited the failure to provide adequate distributor roads, particularly to the north of the developed area, and an incomplete link road via Westerleigh Common (known locally as 'the road to nowhere'). This link across the common had been partly funded by the Stanshawes estate developers, but after 1974 Avon County Council argued that it could not afford to prioritize its completion.[180]

By 1998 the new town development was served by a series of secondary roads. Goose Green Way, extending north from Station Road and bearing west towards Iron Acton, bounded most of the residential area north of the River Frome. Rodford Way, linking Kennedy Way (via Heron Way) in the east to Westerleigh Road in the west, formed the southern boundary of the parish after 1988. It served the new estates south of Station Road, which was still designated the main route through the reconstituted parish.[181]

175 *The Times*, May 1964; pers. comm. YHC; Verey and Brooks, *Glos.* II, 827.
176 Verey and Brooks, *Glos.* II, 826.
177 YHC, D/296; site visit Sept. 2012; Verey and Brooks, *Glos.* II, 829.
178 GA, DA 33/701/3/4; YHC, D/296 (1967).
179 YHC, D/296 (1967).
180 YHC, D/302/1–4 1978.
181 OS Map, 1:25 000 sheet 167 (1998 edn).

MANORS AND ESTATES

YATE MANOR, WHICH EXTENDED over more than 3,000 a. in the north of the ancient parish, was the principal and largest of its three manors; it overlapped Tanhouse Lane in the south and the Chipping Sodbury to Wickwar Road in the east.[1] To its east Brinsham manor, c.300 a., lay on either side of that road at the foot of the limestone ridge, and was bounded by Mapleridge Lane and the Ladden Brook. Stanshawes, another small manor, of c.200 a., lay south of Station Road.[2]

In 1066 and 1086 Yate and Brinsham were both constituents of an estate of the bishops of Worcester centred on Westbury-on-Trym. Thereafter, the manors in Yate were subinfeudated to tenants by the bishops of Worcester. By the mid 16th century, overlordship of these manors had been conveyed to the crown.[3]

Members of the de Willington family held Yate from 1208 to 1397; during the 16th century the Berkeleys leased the manor, transforming the fortified medieval court into a sizeable mansion. Yate Court was destroyed during the Civil Wars, and this misfortune, combined with early inclosure and a series of absentee lords throughout the 17th century, began the manor's fragmentation into larger independent farms.[4] Brinsham, as a predominantly agricultural estate, replaced its mansion in the 16th century with a large farmhouse. A possession of the Burnell family throughout the 16th and 17th centuries, it eventually descended to the Chesters, residents of Knole Park (Almondsbury) and lords of Almondsbury manor.[5] From 1839 the two manors were united under the lordship of the Randolph family, until the division of the estate by sale in 1911–12.

Stanshawes was somewhat distinct from Yate's other manors. In 1086 it was an outlier of Haresfield, a royal demesne in Whitstone hundred, and its lands extended beyond Yate's boundaries into both Wapley and Dodington. The Stanshawe family, who derived their name from the manor, dominated its lordship until c.1500. Although long worked as two estates, Stanshawes Court and Stanshawes Farm, the manor remained a single landholding until its sale in c.1920. Its manor house, somewhat dilapidated by the mid 19th century, was revived by Robert Nathaniel Hooper in 1871.[6]

All three manors remained active farming centres, although they had perhaps diminished as seats of local power by the 18th century. In addition they all looked beyond agriculture for their economic development, notably to the extractive industries; the lords of Yate and Stanshawes manors in particular were quick to capitalise on the rich

---

1   GA, D 1610/E120; GDR, T 1/207.
2   GA, D 674a/P1; GDR, T 1/207.
3   See p. 95.
4   See pp. 27–8.
5   See pp. 31–4.
6   See pp. 34–7.

coal and mineral deposits beneath their farmlands.[7] As wealth and productivity grew in the parish during the 19th century, the manors were consolidated and redeveloped.

Yate

Before and after the Norman Conquest Yate, along with Henbury, Redwick and Stoke Bishop, belonged to the bishop of Worcester's manor of Westbury-on-Trym, in Brentry hundred.[8] By the late 13th century, the manor of Yate was held of the bishop of Worcester by knight service for half a fee.[9] When, in 1547, Nicholas Heath, bishop of Worcester, sold to the crown his estates as delineated in 1086,[10] the overlordship of Yate was not mentioned by name, but no other record of its transfer has been discovered. Overlordship remained with the bishop in 1509, but royal grants of 1555/6 and 1565 confirm that Yate was a crown possession before 1552.[11]

Before 1200 Robert d'Evercy held Yate from the bishop of Worcester by knight's service, along with Ablington in Bibury, and Aston (Worcs.).[12] In 1207 d'Evercy granted these manors to his son-in-law, Ralph de Willington (I).[13] Although Aston reverted to the bishop soon afterwards, successive generations of the de Willingtons held Yate and Ablington.[14]

In 1284–5, Ralph (III) de Willington held Yate for half a knight's fee of the bishop.[15] By 1303 Ralph (III) had been succeeded by John; who still held the manor in 1316, both holding as of the bishop as before.[16] In 1338 John de Willington, great-grandson of Ralph (I), died seised of the manors of Yate and Ablington, along with Frampton Cotterell, Sandhurst, and lands in Poulton (Awre).[17] John had also held Westonbirt manor, which reverted to the Crown in 1321 when the goods of Humphrey de Bohun, overlord of Westonbirt, were confiscated owing to his part in the rebellion of Thomas of Lancaster against Edward II.[18] John's son Ralph (IV) recovered it after 1323, and when he died, c.1348–9, Westonbirt had rejoined Yate and the other manors of the family's Gloucestershire estate.[19]

Ralph (IV) was succeeded by his uncle Reginald, but Yate was held in tail to Ralph's cousin Sir Henry Willington, who owned substantial properties in Gloucestershire and five other counties.[20] Henry's son, Sir John Willington of Umberleigh (Devon), was heir

---

7   See pp. 47–53

8   M. Hollings (ed.), *Red Book of Worcester* (1934) IV, 405.

9   *Feudal Aids*, II, 234.

10   TNA, E 328/43.

11   GA, D 269B/T25; TNA, E 150/343/4; see p. 33.

12   *Red Book of Worcester* IV, 405, 438.

13   *Glos. Feet of Fines 1199–1299*, 11 (no. 64); *VCH Worcs.* III, 557–61.

14   *Glos. Feet of Fines 1199–1299*, 13 (no. 71); *Book of Fees* I, 186–191; *VCH Worcs.* III, 557–61.

15   *Feudal Aids* II, 234.

16   *Feudal Aids*, II, 253, 276.

17   *Inq. p.m. Glos.* 1302–58, 271–3.

18   *VCH Glos.* XI, 285–88; *ODNB* s.a. Bohun, Humphrey (VII) de, 4th earl of Hereford and 9th earl of Essex (c.1276–1322) (accessed 20 March 2015).

19   *Inq. p.m. Glos.* 1302–58, 318–19.

20   Ibid., Henry's father, Henry de Willington (I), was executed at Bristol in 1322 for his part in Lancaster's rebellion against the Despencers, Burke's *Commoners*, vol. 4 (1838), 526

to both his father and to Reginald, and succeeded to his father's estates when aged only seven in 1349–50.[21] John's son Ralph (V) was also a minor when he inherited in 1378,[22] and some years previously John had granted life interests in the manor of Yate and other estates to Sir John Beaumont of Shirwell (Devon), Thomas de Bruthfield and Thomas de Willington, his great uncle.[23]

Ralph (V) died in 1382; his brother John succeeded him but died in royal custody without issue in 1396.[24] With no male heir, John's sisters Isabel and Margaret were co-heiresses of the Willington estates. Isabel, the wife of William Beaumont, Sir John's son, inherited Yate, two-thirds of the manor of Sandhurst, and lands in Westonbirt, Poulton, Culverden, Ablington and Frampton Cotterell.[25] On her death in 1423, Isabel's son Thomas Beaumont, who was reputedly born at Yate, inherited the manor.[26]

The manors of Yate, Westonbirt and Sandhurst descended to Thomas's sons William and then Philip, who died in 1473. Although the inquisition held at Philip's death found John Basset, the husband of Philip's sister Joan, to be the rightful heir, nevertheless by 1483 the three manors were held by Thomas Beaumont, and then his brother Hugh in 1488.[27] In 1501 Hugh settled Yate with Westonbirt, Sandhurst, Frampton Cotterell and Ablington in trust for Giles Daubeney,[28] whose son Sir Henry Daubeney, from 1538 earl of Bridgwater, inherited them in 1509.[29]

The Daubeneys were not resident lords of Yate manor. In 1504 Giles leased it to Maurice Berkeley, whose castle, and many of the family's other estates, had been settled on the crown at the end of the 15th century.[30] A new lease, agreed between Berkeley and Henry Daubeney in 1516, extended the original provision of two lives by an additional 80 years, and thereafter Berkeley began a significant redevelopment of the manor house. Three generations of Berkeleys lived at Yate; although they shared their time between London and estates in Warwickshire, several of their children were born and married from the manor house.[31] In 1565 Henry Berkeley sold the remainder of the lease to Sir Nicholas Poyntz of Iron Acton, his neighbour and relation by marriage.[32]

In 1547 Henry Daubeney sold Yate, Westonbirt and Sandhurst to Edward Seymour, duke of Somerset.[33] After his attainder in 1552, the crown granted Yate and the Gloucestershire manors, formerly under Daubeney's lordship, to James Bassett in 1557, to be held in trust for his nephew Arthur, great-grandson of John Basset.[34] In

---

21   *Inq. p.m. Glos.* 1302–58, 322.
22   *Inq. p.m. Glos.* 1359–1413, 135–6.
23   Ibid.
24   Ibid. 128, 195–6, 201–2; *VCH Glos.* XIII (forthcoming): Sandhurst, manors and estates.
25   *Cal. Close* 1396–9, 165–6; *Cal. Pat.* 1396–9, 263; *VCH Glos.* XIII (forthcoming): Sandhurst, manors and estates.
26   *Cal. Inq. p.m.* XXII, 273–4.
27   TNA, C 140/46/50; *VCH Glos.* XI, 285–88; *VCH Glos.* XIII (forthcoming): Sandhurst, manors and estates.
28   *Glos. Feet of Fines 1360–1508,* 192–4.
29   TNA, C 142/24/54; *Complete Peerage,* II, 311.
30   Berkeley Castle muns. GC 4524 courtesy of H. Lane; *Trans. BGAS,* 21 (1898), 25.
31   Berkeley Castle muns. GC 4524; Smith, *Lives of the Berkeleys* (1883), II, 194–6, 211, 254–5.
32   Smith, *Lives of the Berkeleys,* II, 356; *Visit. Glos. 1623,* 129.
33   TNA, CP 25(2)/66/545 no. 26.
34   GA, D 269B/T25; D 1956/Acc 231.3/box 1/1; see also above note 10.

1579 Arthur sold Westonbirt and Sandhurst to Alexander Neale and James Winston respectively.[35] Yate remained part of his estates, and was inherited by his son Robert in 1585.[36]

A suggestion that Nicholas Damory purchased Yate from the Bassetts shortly after 1557 cannot be confirmed,[37] although he may have held a copyhold tenement in the manor, or even an interest in Brinsham.[38] Damory (also spelled Dimmery and Dymery) was lord of Westonbirt manor, having purchased it in 1593 from Samuel, Alexander Neale's son,[39] and the family was referred to as Damory 'of Yate' at the heralds' visitation in 1623.[40]

A decree in Chancery confirmed the sale of Yate manor by Robert Bassett and his creditors to Edward, viscount Chichester, and his son Arthur in 1634.[41] Bassett, who was alleged to have sold more than 30 manors to discharge considerable debts,[42] had previously used part of his Yate estate to secure loans,[43] and had surrendered 28 tenements there to John May in repayment of debts. May sold them in 1624 to Arthur Chichester, Baron Belfast, who was Edward's brother.[44] In 1638 Edward Chichester spent more than £1,500 on reconsolidating the manorial estate. His purchases included Yate Court and demesnes from Nicholas Bridges, John Blagden and his brothers.[45] The vendors had previously agreed with Bassett to retain an interest in the manor as copyhold tenants for terms of two or three lives.[46]

In 1652 Arthur, Lord Chichester (created Earl of Donegal, 1647), who succeeded Edward in 1648, sold the manor to Sir Dennis Gawden, a London clothier for £6,300.[47] In 1663 he conveyed it to Richard Beckford, a fellow clothier and citizen of London, on a 999-year lease, for a peppercorn rent, thereby repaying a loan of £5,150 which Gawden had borrowed from Beckford.[48] When he died in 1679 Beckford left the manor in trust to his executors, having previously assigned the remaining term of the lease to his son-in-law, Robert Oxwick.[49]

A dispute with the rector after 1710 regarding tithes described Oxwick as lord of the manor;[50] there was another claimant to the title, however, as returns to quarter sessions name Charles William Howard, Earl of Suffolk, as lord in 1719.[51] Suffolk's marriage to Arabella Astry, daughter of Sir Samuel Astry of Henbury, included one-third of the

35   TNA, C 142/209/21; *VCH Glos.* XI, 286; *VCH Glos.* XIII (forthcoming): Sandhurst, manors and estates.
36   TNA, C 142/209/21.
37   E.S. Lindley, 'Manor of Yate', *Trans. BGAS*, 85 (1966), 156–63.
38   GA, D 1923, bundle 8; D1610/E120.
39   *VCH Glos.* XI, 286; GA, D 1956/Acc 231.3/box 2/1.
40   *Visit. Glos. 1623*, 244.
41   GA, D 1923, bundle 13, nos. 17, 24.
42   J. Prince, *Worthies of Devon* (1810 edn), 52.
43   GA, D 1923, bundle 13, doc 32; see also *Hist. Parl. Commons 1604–29*, vol. 3, 630.
44   GA, D 1923, bundle 2, doc 4.
45   GA, D 1923, bundle 13, docs 32, 38.
46   GA, D 1923, bundle 13, docs 15, 30 32; D9125/1/12414.
47   GA, D 1923, bundle 13, doc 42.
48   GA, D 1923, bundle 13, 'Capt. Beckfords deede Concerning the money lent to Mr Gawden'.
49   TNA, PROB 11/361 1679; Cornwall RO, CY/1203 16 Oct. 1677, courtesy of C. Willmore, Yate.
50   See p. 93.
51   GA, Q/SO/4, 227, dated. 1719.

hundred of Henbury in the settlement, and this may have formed the basis for his claim to lordship of Yate.[52] Suffolk notwithstanding, Oxwick bequeathed the manor by will dated 1724 to his nephew, Robert Kendall, later Sir Robert Cater. Cater predeceased Oxwick, and the manor passed to Cater's widow Mary in 1740.[53]

In 1757 Sir Francis Knollis, Cater's son-in-law, held the manor,[54] which passed, after his widow's death in 1791, to Beckford Cater of Essex.[55] When he died in 1806 his grand-daughters, Francis Spencer and Mary Cater, and their brother-in-law, Richard Sherbourne, inherited equal shares of the manor.[56] Mary bequeathed her holdings to her cousin's husband, Revd Henry Jones Randolph of Hawkesbury, with the reversion of her brother-in-law's and sister's shares, and the manor of Brinsham.[57]

From 1839 until 1923 lordship of both Yate and Brinsham manors descended in the Randolph family.[58] The manor's significance had largely disappeared by 1911–12, when the last lord, Henry de Beaumont Randolph, who lived in Ontario (Canada), divided and sold the manor lands; he continued to assert lordship, however, by reserving mineral rights in the conditions of sale.[59]

Yate Court and the Lands of the Manor

The medieval manor house, which stood at the southern end of a deer park established between 1254 and 1303,[60] was granted a license to crenulate in 1299. It was surrounded by a moat, enclosing a rectangle c.91 x c.73 m.[61] By c.1321, the demesne lands also included rabbit warrens and a windmill.[62]

After 1516 Maurice Berkeley employed local craftsmen and stone quarried locally to rebuild the manor house.[63] According to Smith, the Berkeleys' chronicler, 'such was this lords liking to his seate at Yate' he sold off many of his other properties outside the county, and bought holdings within the vicinity, 'declaring himself thereby to bee a reall Gloucestershire man'.[64]

A survey of 1548–9 described the court as 220 feet long by 150 feet wide, walled with rough stone and embattled. There was a chapel within the complex, and a lodge and gatehouse on its perimeter.[65] The park, enclosed within a wall and pale, encompassed 2½ miles (4 km) by estimation, and included a dovecote, warrens and a corn mill with

52   GA, D 2957/160/218. Peerage ref. for his accession to title 1718.
53   TNA, PROB 11/708/134.
54   GA, Q/SO/8; Burke, *Genealogical and Heraldic History of the Extinct and Dormant Baronetcies of England* (1838), 293.
55   GA, Q/SO/9 and 11.
56   *Gents. Mag.* LXXVI pt. 1 (1806), 584; GA, Q/SO/12; *VCH Beds.* III, 296–305.
57   TNA, PROB 11/1868/439.
58   TNA, PROB 11/1915/327; GDR, T 1/207; *Kelly's Dir. Glos.* (1906 edn), 371–2; (1923 edn), 379.
59   GA, D 6822/70; *Kelly's Dir. Glos.* (1906 edn), 371–2; (1923 edn), 379; YHC, Sale Particulars, 1911.
60   *Cal. Pat. 1301–7*, 184; GA, D 2762/T14, 27 June 1254; Lay and Isles, 'Medieval Deer Parks', 9.
61   *Cal. Pat. 1291–1301*, 430; *Trans. BGAS*, 21 (1898), 8–12.
62   *Cal. Chart. 1300–26*, 165; TNA, E 142/24; below, p. 42.
63   See above; also YHC, MF facsimile Berkeley Castle Muns., general series book 28, for example ff. 165–9 (1519).
64   Smith, *Lives of the Berkeleys*, 196; below, pp. 67–8.
65   *Trans. BGAS*, 21 (1898) 22–4.

Figure 6 *Ruins of the Great Hall at Yate Court, c.1920.*

millpond.[66] The near-contemporary Yate Court farmhouse stood close to the mansion on its south-west side.[67]

In 1644 Parliamentary forces were garrisoned there, and on their retreat razed the manor house to the ground.[68] In 1659 the former manorial complex, by then a tenement of approximately 241 a., was referred to as Blagden's Court, after its tenant John Blagden, who held it for three lives from Bassett.[69]

In 1722 Robert Oxwick constructed a new mansion, Oxwick House, just east of the site of Yate Court, but by the early 19th century this had been demoted to a farmhouse.[70] Before 1829 the Cater family built Yate House as their manorial seat in the east of the parish, south of Yate Rocks, and it was adopted by the Randolph family when they acquired the manor.[71]

Both the Yate Court complex and Oxwick House were sold as part of the 'Yate House Estate' in 1911, and continued as working farms into the 20th century.[72] Yate House had been leased to Francis F. Fox before 1889[73] and remained a private residence until at least

66 *Trans. BGAS*, 21 (1898) 22–4.
67 NHL, no. 1312280, Yate Court farmhouse: 12 Feb. 2015.
68 HER S. Glos. no. 18027; *Bibliotheca Glos.* 129–30.
69 GA, D 1610/E120; D 9125/1/12414; above, note 43.
70 HER S. Glos. no. 2891; GDR, T 1/207.
71 TNA, PROB 11/1868/439; *Kelly's Dir. Glos.* (1879 edn), 793; *Census,* 1861; see p. 33.
72 GA, D 6822/70; TNA, MAF 73/14/69; see pp. 42–4.
73 *Kelly's Dir. Glos.* (1889, 1906, 1927, 1931 edns); GA, D2428/1/86, 133.

Figure 7 *Oxwick House, built c.1722, to replace Yate Court as the manorial seat (photographed c.1910).*

the 1930s.[74] In 1984 it was described as an inn but by 2012, renamed Rockwood House, it had been subdivided into apartments.[75] By then Yate Court farmhouse and Oxwick 'farmhouse' were both private dwellings.[76]

A survey in 1659, during Dennis Gawden's lordship, computed the manor of Yate as 3,447 a., of which 618 were commons; the demesne and copyhold tenements accounted for *c.*1,996 a., and the remainder, *c.* 832 a., was made up of freeholds and highways.[77]

The freehold estates are less well documented. Before 1626 Thomas Burnell (II), lord of Brinsham manor, and his brother Henry, held several land parcels formerly within the manor of Yate.[78] In 1640 Arthur, Lord Chichester, mortgaged the manor of Yate, repaying the debt in 1650. To pay off the mortgage he sold 12 copyhold tenements, of between *c.*20 a. and more than 80 a., to their then occupiers and other local gentlemen. Chichester retained fee farm rents on the properties he sold, and royalties on any coal extracted from the land.[79] These sales began a pattern of land transfer within the manor that led to the development of substantial farming estates and mining operations in the 18th and 19th centuries.[80]

74 *Kelly's Dir. Glos.* (1889, 1906, 1927, 1931, 1939 edns).
75 NHL, no. 1312292, Rockwood House: 12 Feb. 2015; HER S. Glos. no. 9664.
76 Local inf.; NHL, no. 1321124, Rockwood House: 12 Feb. 2015.
77 GA, D 1610/E120.
78 *Inq. p.m. Glos.* 1625–36, 19–22.
79 GA, D 1923, bundle 13, docs 13, 20, 23, 24; Cornwall RO, CY/1200, copy made 1805, courtesy of C. Willmore, Yate; *ODNB* s.a. Chichester, Arthur, first earl of Donegal [Donegall] (1606–75) (accessed 19 Feb. 2015).
80 See pp. 42–5.

In 1838 Henry Jones Randolph's combined holdings in the parish from his manors of Brinsham and Yate exceeded 1,000 a.[81] When the whole estate was sold in 1911–12 in 40 lots the Brinsham (51 a. and 94 a.) and Yate Court (255 a.) lots largely corresponded to the former demesne lands.[82] Much former manorial land continued to be farmed as individual holdings into the 20th century; several farms were bought by companies seeking to exploit the parish's mineral wealth, who maintained agricultural production by tenants alongside stone and celestine extraction.[83]

Brinsham

Brinsham, like Yate, was part of the estates of the bishops of Worcester, and is first mentioned in a charter of 990, whereby Bishop Oswald granted the enclosure or *'worthig'* of *'Brynes hamme'* to Aethelm.[84] In 1166 Sampson de Saltmarsh (Salsomar or Salso Marisco) held Brinsham of the bishop with estates in Lawrence Weston and Southmead (Bristol), which also lay within the episcopal manor of Westbury.[85] Brinsham descended with the Saltmarshs until at least 1254. [86] In 1303 Stephen de Saltmarsh held Brinsham, Lawrence Weston and Southmead of the bishop by knight service for half a fee.[87] Stephen witnessed a grant of the manor of Manchester (Lancs.), made at Wickwar in 1309, and had royal commission in 1312 but died before 1316 when his widow, Alice, was wife of John de Bradley.[88] He was succeeded in Brinsham by his son, also Stephen, who held the manor in 1346.[89]

Stephen's heir, Joan, held the manor with her husband, John Paunton, in 1393. They let the manor to John Glastonbury and Isabel his wife for a life term in 1401 with reversion to Joan and John and Joan's heirs.[90] Joan married at least three times. In 1407 manor courts acknowledged William Goodfellow (d. *c.*1412) as lord of Brinsham by right of marriage.[91] After John Goodfellow's death, Joan married William Gore and he presided over the manor courts.[92] The manor was held in tail to the heirs of Joan by John Goodfellow,[93] so that for much of the 15th century the Goodfellow family dominated the manor court rolls: Thomas Goodfellow and his wife Margaret, presided over the court with William Peers between 1433 and 1434; and John Goodfellow sat with Robert Poyntz, Thomas Fetypas and Nicholas Stanshawe, feoffees of the manor, between 1436 and 1446.[94]

81 GDR, T 1/207.
82 GA, D 6822/70; P. Alcock, *Remember Your Manors* (1996).
83 P. Alcock, *Remember Your Manors* (1996); TNA, MAF 73/14/69; *Kelly's Dir. Glos.* (1906, 1914, 1931 edns).
84 Finberg, *Early Charters*, 63 (no. 136).
85 M. Hollings (ed), *Red Book of Worcester* (1934) IV, 413, 436–9.
86 Ibid. 439; GA, D 2762/T14, 27 June 1254.
87 *Feudal Aids*, II, 253.
88 *Chetham Soc. Misc.* IX (Manchester, 1841), 249; *Cal. Pat.* 1307–13, 476; *Feudal Aids*, II, 276.
89 Feudal Aids, II, 289.
90 *Glos. Feet of Fines 1360–1508*, 60, 72; see also GA, D 674a/M27, rot. 1, pt. 7, 4 Apr. 1407.
91 GA, D 674a/M27, rot. 1, 1407–12.
92 *Glos. Feet of Fines 1360–1508*, 87–8; also GA, D 674a/M27, rot. 2, 1413–19.
93 *Glos. Feet of Fines 1360–1508*, 79.
94 GA, D 674a/M27, rot. 3, pts. 9–14, 1433–46.

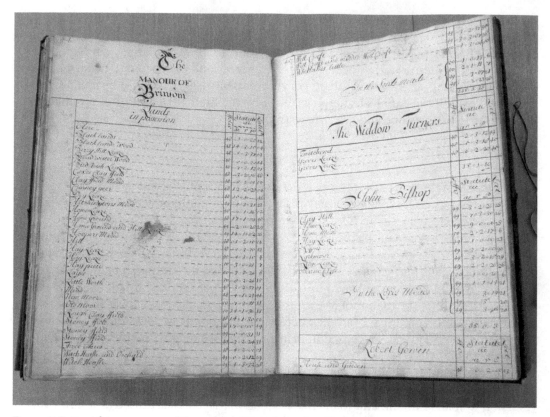

Figure 8 *Extract from a survey of the manor of Brinsham, detailing the demesne and two of the tenants'*
holdings, c.1700.

Subsequently no lord is referred to until Thomas Burnell (I) in 1540, who held the
manor of Brinsham of Ralph Sadleir by knight service as of his manor of Henbury (as
successor to the bishops of Worcester) for a fee of 11*d*., annually.[95] By royal grant made
before 1587, Sadleir held the 'whole college of Westbury-on-Trym' and 'the Hundred
Liberties and Franchises of Henbury', also formerly part of the episcopal estate.[96]

Successive generations of the Burnells continued as lords until at least 1682.[97] The
family also held several tenements in Yate, held of that manor in socage by fealty, suit at
court and 2*s*. rent per annum; and lands formerly part of the manor held independently
of the king in chief. Thomas (II), who also held ten tenements in Chipping Sodbury,
including a house and tanhouse,[98] succeeded his father before 1614,[99] but granted the
manor to his father's widow, Elizabeth, for 99 years or life. She was still living when he

95   GA, D 674a/M28 draft roll, 1540, GA, D 674a/M29 draft roll, 1544; *Inq. p.m. Glos.* 1625–36, 19–22,
     121–2; Duke Univ. Lib. Ovsz Box 18 (survey, 1608), f. 3.

96   F.S. Stoney, *Memoir of the Life and Times of Sir R. Sadleir* (1877) 243–6.

97   GA, D 674a/M30, 1605–1682.

98   *Inq. p.m. Glos.* 1625–36, 19–22, 121–2.

99   Ibid.

died in 1626.[100] Thomas (III) succeeded his father, but died in 1631, and his brother Robert inherited.[101]

In 1681 Thomas Burnell (IV) held the manor, as well as 'messuage gardens orchards lands and common pasture in Yate, Brinsham, Chipping Sodbury and Olde Sodbury'.[102] He married Elizabeth Chester before 1686, but died without issue, leaving the manor to his brother-in-law, Thomas Chester of Knole Park (Almondsbury).[103] Brinsham remained a property of the Chester family for the rest of the 18th century, although Knole Park was their principal residence.

In c.1770 William Bromley Chester was lord of Brinsham, as well as of the manors of Barton Regis, Almondsbury and Brockenborrow.[104] Thomas Master, cousin of William's widow, Elizabeth Bromley Chester, inherited the manor in 1799, along with the Chester estates in Almondsbury and Barton Regis.[105] In 1814 Thomas Master and William Chester-Master placed these estates in trust; the trustees were charged with selling the manors, including Brinsham.[106] By 1829 Mary Cater of Yate Manor held Brinsham, and left both to her cousin's husband, Henry Jones Randolph. The manor of Brinsham descended with Yate from 1836 until both estates were sold in 1911–12.[107]

The Brinsham manor estate was concentrated in the east of the parish, but as late as the 18th century it continued to hold lands in Yate manor.[108] A partial demarcation of Yate and Brinsham lands resulted from a dispute in 1254 between their respective lords, Ralph de Willington and John de Saltmarsh. They agreed that Yate manor would retain lands east of the Sodbury to Wickwar road, from (*Bishopshulle*) Bishops Hill Wood to (*Mapelduredge*) Mapleridge Lane. In return John de Saltmarsh won rights to common pasture throughout the fields and woods south of Mapleridge Lane, bounded by the Ladden Brook, but relinquished any claim to access the park and certain open fields within Yate manor.[109]

In 1700 the manor encompassed 357 a., of which 248 a. were demesne lands.[110] A later survey, of 1767, estimated the manor at 341 a.; by then the demesne had been divided into two tenements of c.53 a. and c.161 a., held by Sarah and Nathaniel Corbett (also Corbitt) respectively.[111]

Brinsham farmhouse, built in the late 16th or early 17th century, probably occupies the site of the original mansion.[112] The house was extended during the 19th century, establishing a second wing set back and to the right of the original L-plan farmhouse.

100 *Inq. p.m. Glos.* 1625–36, 121–2.
101 *Inq. p.m. Glos.* 1625–36, 19–22, 121–2.
102 TNA, CP 25/2/659/33 ChasIIMich.
103 R.E. Chester Waters, *Genealogical Memoirs of the Families of Chester* (1881), 37.
104 GA, Q/SO/7–9; TNA, CP 25/2/1316/16 and 17; Rudder, *Glos.* 224. Brockenborrow was a manor, now lost, within the parish of Almondsbury.
105 GA, D 674a; Q/SO/10; Q/SO/ 12.
106 GA, D 674a/F18 11 Aug. 1814.
107 See p. 31.
108 See pp. 30–1.
109 GA, D 2762/T14, 27 June 1254.
110 GA, D 674a/P1.
111 GA, D 674a/E40.
112 HER S. Glos. no. 2086, P. Jones, *Parish Survey* (1978); NHL, no. 1137493, Brinsham farmhouse, including attached barn and cartshed: 12 Feb. 2015; GA, D 6822/70.

The 18th-century farm buildings, adjoining the house to the east, comprise a barn, stables and cart shed.[113] Little Brinsham Farm, built after c.1650, stands just south of Brinsham farmhouse and is a more modest building with a dairy to the rear, stables and outbuildings.[114]

After Yate and Brinsham manors were sold in 1911–12, the two holdings formed out of the demesne lands continued as working farms. In 1933 Brinsham Farm was bought by British Quarries Ltd, who continued to let it until 1996. Although quarrying continued nearby, Brinsham operated as a dairy farm until 1974.[115]

Stanshawes

The manor of Stanshawes in Yate was an outlier of Haresfield in Whitstone hundred. In 1086 Haresfield was royal demesne under the superintendence of the sheriff of Gloucestershire, Durand of Gloucester.[116] In 1235 Herbert fitz Herbert (great-grandson of Durand's son, Miles of Gloucester), held three knight's fees of the king, including Stanshaw park, '*Parco Stanchawe*'.[117] Herbert was succeeded by his brother Reginald and died in 1286, seised of one-third of the manor of Haresfield, and the rent of assize of '*Stanschawes*' of 20s.[118] Stanshawes remained in the service of Haresfield in 1412,[119] but by the early 16th century the manor was held of the lord of Yate, Henry, Lord Daubeney.[120]

A freehold in eastern Gloucestershire, which descended with the manors of Hempton and Brockenborrow in Almondsbury parish, was also known as 'Stanshawes', and has been confused with the manor in Yate.[121] This freehold probably derived from a family name, since Stanshaws held Hempton manor by 1435.[122] In 1593 Thomas Ivye died seised of the manors of Brockenborrow and 'Stanshawes in Hempton',[123] and throughout the 17th century this 'Stanshawes' descended with Brockenborrow manor.[124] It was claimed c.1715 that the house and demesnes were known as 'Standshall-court',[125] but before 1800 Brockenborrow was considered a 'lost' manor.[126]

The (de) Stanshawe family, who allegedly derived their name from the manor in Yate, held the lordship there for more than 200 years.[127] In 1262 the abbot of St Augustine's, Bristol, brought a suit of novel disseisin against Adam de Stanshawe regarding the abbey's

---

113 NHL, no. 1137493, Brinsham farmhouse: 12 Feb. 2015; GA, D 6822/70 map.

114 NHL, no. 1321122, Little Brinsham farmhouse: 12 Feb. 2015; GA, D 6822/70.

115 *Kelly's Dir. Glos.* (1914, 1923, 1931 edns); TNA, MAF 73/14/69; P. Alcock, *Remember Your Manors*, 47–51.

116 *Domesday*, 452; B. Coplestone-Crow, 'A Grant of Lands in the Manor of Wallstone', *Gwent Local History: the Journal of Gwent Local History Council*, 87 (1999), 5.

117 *Book of Fees*, I (1920), 439.

118 *Inq. p.m. Glos.* 1236–1300, 132–4.

119 *Inq. p.m. Glos.* 1359–1413, 264–5.

120 TNA, C 142/35/8.

121 Rudder, *Glos.* 224.

122 *Inq. p.m. Glos.* 1359–1413, 264–5.; TNA, CP 40/639, rot. 107d; *Cal. Close* 1435–41, 9–12.

123 TNA, C 142/237/136.

124 Trans. *BGAS*, 17 (1892–3), 228; CP 43/508, rot. 28.

125 Atkyns, *Glos.* 246.

126 GA, D 674a/T14, 1622; Rudder, *Glos.* 224; *PN Glos.* III, 106.

127 Coplestone-Crow, 'Grant of Lands'.

Figure 9 *View of Stanshawes Court from the lawn, c.1910.*

tenement within the manor.[128] According to an inquisition of 1412, Isabel Stanshawe had five years earlier bequeathed the Stanshawes manor, described as lying 'in the vills of Chepyngsobbury, Oldesobbury and Yate' to her eldest son Robert, who duly occupied it.[129]

The Stanshawe family held the manor until *c.*1500. Robert Stanshawe, son of Robert and his wife Isabel, the daughter of Robert Poyntz of Iron Acton, died in 1473 seised of lands in Wapley, Dodington and Yate, and the manor of Alderley.[130] Although his inquisition did not refer directly to Stanshawes, in 1470 he had bequeathed a bell to St Mary's church, Yate, as 'skhyer' [squire] of Stanshawes manor.[131] The manor probably descended with Alderley on Robert's death, but his son and heir, Thomas, relinquished his claim to Alderley, granting it instead to Robert Poyntz.[132] When Poyntz died in 1521 his Gloucestershire possessions included the manors of Iron Acton, Alderley and Stanshawes, which he held of Henry Daubeney, lord of Yate manor.[133]

Between 1542 and 1546 John Poyntz (Robert's heir) and his son Nicholas conveyed the manor to John Smyth, mayor and alderman of Bristol.[134] Smyth granted the manor

128 *Cal. Close* 1261–4, 171–4.
129 *Inq. p.m. Glos.* 1359–1413, 264–5.; YHC, D/2051.
130 GA, D 1086/T2/26; *Visit. Glos. 1623*, 132.
131 *Trans. BGAS*, 18 (1893–4), 240.
132 GA, D 1086/T2/16.
133 TNA, C 142/35/8.
134 TNA, CP 25/2/14/82/31 HenVIIIEast; CP 25/2/14/83/38 HenVIIIMich.

in *c.*1556 to his second son Matthew,[135] who sold it to Christopher Stokes in 1561.[136] The Stokes family of Seend (Wilts.) were successful clothiers who had consequently achieved gentry status; they retained estates in Wiltshire, along with Stanshawes, and had interests in the neighbouring parish of Wickwar.[137] By the end of the 18th century the family no longer lived in the parish and the manor house was let.[138] They retained the manor, however, and were among the largest landowners in the parish until they sold Stanshawes to Robert Nathaniel Hooper in 1871.[139]

The manor's extent is hard to determine, as it appeared to overlap parish boundaries. In Yate in 1473 it comprised 3 messuages, 20 a. of land, 20 a. of pasture, and 15 a. of meadow. Robert Stanshawe also held 2 virgates of land, 4 a. of pasture and 6 a. of meadow in Dodington, and 2 messuages, 58 a. of pasture, 23 a. of arable and 3 a. of wood in Wapley.[140] In 1603–4 a dispute arose regarding tithes due from Stanshawes to the church at Yate, and evidence was presented which suggested that the manor included parts of Dodington; perambulations of both parishes impinged on its lands, and at least 6 a. of its meadow lay outside Yate. Almost all deponents confirmed, however, that the Stanshawes tenants attended church at Yate.[141]

The estate included Stanshawes Court (the manor house), Stanshawes farm and a chapel; from the 18th century there was also a limekiln and coal mines 'about' the manor, in addition to the farmlands and orchards.[142] In 1841 it was divided between two holdings, *c.*200 a. in total.[143] Before its sale to Hooper in 1871 the manor house was 'in ruins'; he redeveloped it as a substantial manor house in transitional Early English style, with extensive gardens, partially enclosed by a serpentine wall.[144] Hooper died in 1914, and in the following years the manor was divided and sold as three estates: the Court and two farms: Sergeant's and Stanshawes.[145]

Stanshawes Court continued as a private residence after its sale, but was vacated between 1927 and 1931 and remained empty until 1939 or later.[146] In the Second World War soldiers were billeted there, and it then became a home for Belgian evacuees. Somewhat dilapidated, the house was renovated in the 1960s and converted into a hotel.[147] In 2012 Stanshawes Court continued as a public house.[148]

135 BRO, AC/D/3/49; TNA, C 142/107/52.

136 BRO, AC/D/3/57.

137 A. Schomberg, *The Pedigree of John Stokes of Seend, Co. Wilts* (1886); *VCH Wilts.* VII, 114–21.

138 GA, Q/SO/ 7, 8, 9, 10; GDR, T 1/207; Fitzherbert Brooke inscription in church.

139 GDR, T 1/207; A.P. Stokes, *Stokes Records; notes regarding the ancestry and lives of Anson Phelps Stokes and Helen Louisa (Phelps) Stokes* (1910); *Post Office Dir. Glos.* (1856 edn), 394; *Kelly's Dir. Glos.* (1879 edn), 793.

140 GA, D 1086/T2/26.

141 GDR vol. 89, 395 Baynham *v* Jurden 1603/4.

142 Ibid.; *Wilts. N&Q*, VI (1908–10), 50.

143 GDR, T 1/207.

144 Stokes, *Stokes Records*, 45; *Kelly's Dir. Glos.* (1879 edn), 793; Verey and Brooks, *Glos.* II, 829; site visit 2012.

145 Mon. in church; Eng. Heritage Archives (Swindon), SC 01612; below, pp. 45–6.

146 *Kelly's Dir. Glos.* (1927, 1931, 1939 edns).

147 P. Alcock, *Remember Your Manors*; Verey and Brooks, *Glos.* II, 829.

148 Site visit, 2012.

Like Yate and Brinsham, Stanshawes' mineral wealth attracted enterprises other than farming. Small-scale celestine extraction had been undertaken on the estate during Nathaniel Hooper's lordship, and after 1920 the Bristol Mineral and Land Company bought parts of the land attached to the Court for more extensive excavations.[149] Once these were worked out the area was among the first to be developed under the New Town plan in the 1960s.[150]

149 YHC, parish records 1884; TNA, MAF 73/14/69; below, pp. 51–3.
150 See pp. 64–7.

ECONOMIC HISTORY

Introduction

FOR MUCH OF ITS HISTORY farming dominated economic activity in Yate. Pastoral farming, and dairying in particular, was widely practised from the 13th century or earlier until *c.*1900. Between *c.*1600 and 1750 substantial freehold farms were established, after successive absentee lords fragmented Yate manor, and so encouraged inclosure by private agreement. The owners of these new farming estates were among the first to exploit the parish's significant mineral wealth.[1]

Coal and limestone were worked on a small scale alongside agricultural production from the late 16th century or earlier, supporting local construction and lime-burning. More extensive coal working began before 1800, thus establishing Yate as part of the Bristol coalfield, which was served by the Bristol and Gloucester Railway from 1844.[2] The improved infrastructure gave easier access to Bristol's markets and docks, thus stimulating quarrying operations after 1850. Deposits of celestine found throughout much of the central area of the parish proved a unique and lucrative feature of the local economy. Celestine and limestone extraction continued throughout the 20th century, long after the collieries had closed.

With its strong transport infrastructure and undeveloped space close to Bristol, Yate was considered ideal as a site for growing manufactories. From *c.*1916 the foundation of two factories in the parish changed its economic and demographic structure. Local production drew in a new workforce, and made the growing township a suitable candidate for post-war expansion: a self-sustaining local economy was considered vital to the development of a new town.[3]

The Medieval Period

Although Yate in the medieval period lay within the forest of Horwood, land clearance and cultivation had begun much earlier in what would become the parish. The earliest indications are pre-Roman enclosures in the east of the parish near Brinsham and Birdsbush, and Iron Age field systems near Yate Court and at Hall End in the north-west. Evidence of Roman ironworking and cultivation was found during excavation of the Roman settlement at Hall End.[4]

---

1   See pp. 47–53.
2   J. Cornwell, *Collieries of Kingswood and South Glos.* (1983), 4; see pp. 8–10.
3   See pp. 54–9.
4   HER S. Glos. no. 3063, 7368; see p. 11.

Piecemeal clearance and cultivation continued into the medieval period. In 1190 and 1208 Robert d'Evercy and Ralph de Willington, lords of the manor of Yate, were fined for illegal cutting and assarting within Horwood forest.[5] Traces of medieval ridge and furrow have been located around the manorial seats of Brinsham and Stanshawes, and near Hillhouse Farm in the north-east of the parish; a series of strip lynchets has also been identified on part of the former demesne lands west of Yate Court.[6]

After royal permission was given for disafforestation in 1228, local manorial lords reached agreement to assart and inclose parts of the forest for cultivation.[7] By 1254 clearings for open arable fields and pastures had been made in the woodlands in the north and east of the parish.[8] The de Willingtons at Yate Court inclosed c.350 a. within their manor to create a deer park in the latter half of the 13th century. It perhaps existed as early as 1254, when John de Saltmarsh (lord of the manor of Brinsham) relinquished his right to enter the 'park of Yate',[9] or by 1299 when the court was crenellated;[10] it certainly existed by 1303, when deer poachers were prosecuted.[11] Part of the park was inclosed and converted to meadow shortly before 1548, but 40 deer were also recorded, suggesting that the Berkeley family, then resident at Yate Court, retained some parkland.[12] It was not disparked until after 1600.[13]

Significant areas of woodland remained in 1254, when Yate and Brinsham manors shared common of pasture in Hale Wood, Bircheholte, Mapleridge Wood and Shortwood at Bishops Hill, all in the north and east of the parish.[14] Although not recorded until later, fieldnames such as 'Wooderys', 'Brake', and 'the Dingley' suggest that woodland extended south and west of this area, primarily along the parish's eastern boundary and west toward the centre of Yate.[15]

Access to woodland formed an important part of the local economy. Tenants of the manors used the woods to pasture 'all manner of animals', notably pigs, although the admittance of goats was restricted.[16] Between 1384 and 1412 the Brinsham manor court rolls record the income from sales of wood, numerous fines levied for the illegal cutting and sale of trees and underwood, and dues for pannage.[17]

In c.1320 the demesne of Yate manor totalled more than 500 a., including the court and garden with curtilage, 34 a. of meadow and 32 a. of pasture, 69 a. of woodland, and closes of common pasture. The lord kept cows, sheep and oxen; there was a water mill and a windmill, as well as fishponds and rabbit warrens.[18]

5   Pipe R. 1190 (P.R.S. v. 39), 57; 1208 (P.R.S. v. 61), 22.

6   HER S. Glos. no. 18973, 17548, 5272, 19774.

7   *Cal. Chart.* I, 75; *VCH Glos.* II, 264 and n. 12.

8   GA, D 2762/T14.

9   Ibid.

10   S. Lay and R. Iles, 'Medieval Deer Parks in Avon', *Avon Past,* 1 (1979), 9.

11   *Cal. Pat.* 1301–7, 184.

12   *Trans. BGAS,* 21 (1898), 22–4; see p. 43.

13   See p. 43.

14   GA, D 2762/T14.

15   GDR, T 1/207.

16   GA, D 2762/T14; D 674a/M27.

17   GA, D 674a/M27.

18   TNA, E 142/24, d. 1321–2; *Cal. Chart.* 1300–26, 165; *Cal. Pat.* 1327–30, 76; HER S. Glos. no. 5795.

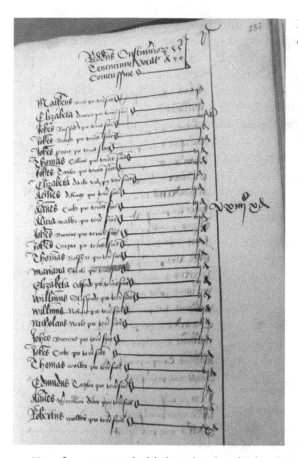

Figure 10 *Detail from a rental listing the tenants of the manor of Yate, c.1552.*

Two free tenants held their lands of John de Willington by knight's service in 1321;[19] William Chesterton held a half-virgate, and William de Denham a farundell (quarter-virgate).[20] In the same year there were 36 other free tenants. Seven held a mondayland (in return for Monday work), but four of these had additional holdings, ranging from 6 to 30 a.; four held a farundell and one a half-virgate. The remaining 20 tenants had holdings from 25 a. down to a single acre, and one held a cottage without land. Fifteen of the free tenants owed works to the lord, in addition to or in lieu of rents. The total value of their holdings was £7 1s. 9d., and the works were valued at £1 5s., or 2d. *per capita*. There were also 35 villein tenants, five holding a half-virgate and 30 a farundell, as well as nine cottagers. Services owed to the lord of Yate manor included mowing hay, harvesting corn and carriage.

A later survey of *c.*1552 also lists two free tenants in the manor of Yate, including Simon Burnell of Brinsham, but the customary tenants had increased to 53; all but six paid 'common fine' or 'head silver' to the lord. In addition to their strips of arable in two open fields, Northfield and Upfield, and of meadow in Cowmead and Hallmead (the

---

19   This para, TNA, E 142/24.
20   In Glos. the size of a yardland (virgate) could vary from 30–60 a.: B. Wells-Furby, *Berkeley Estate, 1281–1417* (2012), 92–4.

lord's meadow), many tenants also held closes, and some of these inclosures remained in the same holdings in 1842.[21]

In 1473 Robert Stanshawe's 55 a. holding in Yate included 20 a. of pasture and 15 a. of meadow, beside other land in Dodington and Wapley; but there is no other evidence for the early structure of Stanshawes manor.[22] Until 1605 there is no detailed delination of the Brinsham tenantry. Between 1384 and 1412 its manor court rolls refer to only two free tenants; the rest were customary tenants. The demesne included pasture and meadow, some arable land for corn, orchards and fisheries. There is also evidence of intercommoning by tenants of Yate and Brinsham manors.[23] In 1605 the manor included two free tenants, twelve customary tenants and a single leaseholder.[24]

A Yate tithing custumal of c.1584 described the range of production across all three manors in the parish. Tithes were due on cows, sheep, pigs and geese, as well as hay and corn. Dairying and textile production were reflected in payments in lieu of milk, cheese and wool,[25] and animal husbandry also supported two tanners.[26] Coal and limestone were being worked in the parish, although no precedents or customs existed regarding the church's right to tax these commodities.[27]

Coal was dug in the area of the royal forest from the 13th century, and it is likely that small-scale excavations took place in Yate before the earliest reference to coal working there in 1584.[28] Local stone was in use before c.1550, not only for building,[29] but also for lime.[30] There is evidence that lime dressing was used to good effect on Yate's pasture and meadowland before 1800.[31] Because the wood and coal needed to fuel the kilns were available locally, as well as suitable stone, lime-burning continued at Yate well into the 19th century.[32]

Markets

Ralph de Willington obtained a grant to hold a market on his manor of Yate in 1218,[33] a few weeks after an almost identical grant had been secured by William Crassus (also Le Gras) of Sodbury.[34] After 1200 royal grants were made on condition that they would not damage existing markets and fairs, and the holding of two markets so close together would place them in direct competition; it is unlikely, therefore, that a market at Yate was successfully established. Because of Henry III's minority, the grants made to both lords in

21   TNA, E 164/39; GDR, T 1/207; see below, pp. 42–3.
22   GA, D 1086/T2/26.
23   GA, D 674a/M27.
24   GA, D 674a/M30.
25   GA, D 1925/2/6742.
26   GDR wills, 1553/76, 1556/2.
27   GA, D 9125/2/6742; GDR vol. 89 p. 395.
28   GA, D 1925/2/6742; *VCH Glos.* II, 235; see p. 45.
29   See p. 45.
30   GDR wills, 1582/33; E. Taylor, 'Limekilns in Avon', *BIAS Journal*, 17 (1984), 5–8.
31   GA, D 674a/E 1767.
32   See pp. 48–9.
33   *Rot. Litt. Claus.* I, 370.
34   *Rot. Litt. Claus.* I, 368.

1218 were only for life,[35] and Crassus obtained a second grant in 1227 for himself and his heirs to hold a weekly market (as well as an annual fair) at Sodbury.[36] No second grant was made to the lords of Yate.

Mills

A watermill and a windmill were recorded as part of the demesne of the manor of Yate in 1321.[37] The windmill was included in the estates of John de Willington at his death in 1338,[38] but latterly mention was only made of water-powered mills. The mill at Yate was described as a 'lyttle corn mylle' served by a 'fayer large mylle pond' in 1548;[39] it probably stood immediately west of Yate Court in Mill Croft, on the Ladden Brook.[40] The watermill was still in use in 1619 and 1638, but no reference is made to it thereafter.[41]

The 17th and 18th Centuries

Agriculture

Between 1600 and 1800 several parts of Yate manor were leased or sold; this fragmentation altered its structure, and the general pattern of landholding within the parish. Before 1624 the lord, Robert Bassett, had granted away various parts of the manor, including the demesne, to pay his debts.[42] Edward, Viscount Chichester, partially reconstituted it but his son, Arthur (latterly Lord Chichester and Earl of Donegal) in 1650 sold *c.*12 copyhold tenements (or parts thereof) of between 20 a. and 80 a.. Most were bought by their former customary tenants.[43] After 1663 Richard Beckford held the manor, and continued this pattern of land transfer through further sales.[44]

The Belsire estate illustrates how large, independent, farming enterprises developed through consolidating these sales. In 1650 Gabriel Belsire paid Arthur, Lord Chichester, £150 for his father's copyhold tenement. A little over 80 a., the holding was almost identical to that held by Thomas Belsire in 1552.[45] It included 5 a. pasture, 34 a. meadow, 22½ a. arable land, 'colepitts' and 'colemynes', and lay west from the church to the parish boundary. Between 1675 and 1708 Gabriel, and his son Richard on his inheritance, bought up several other copyhold tenements in the west of Yate, not only from the manor, but also land previously sold by Beckford to John Millard, John Crowther and others.[46] Richard's farming and domestic activities between 1678 and 1684 are recorded

35   S. Letters, 'Full introduction', *Online Gazetteer of Markets and Fairs in England Wales to 1516* (http:// www.history.ac.uk/cmh/gaz/gazweb2.html).
36   *Cal. Chart*. I, 43.
37   TNA, E 142/24.
38   TNA, C 135/54/5.
39   *Trans. BGAS*, 21 (1898), 24.
40   GDR, T1/207; GA, Q/RI/164.
41   GA, D1086/T87; D1923, bundle 13, no. 32.
42   See p. 27.
43   GA, D 1923, bundles nos. 2, 8, 13 (sale of copyhold tenements under Chichester).
44   GA, D 1923, bundle no. 17 (sales under Beckford); see p. 27.
45   Cornwall RO, CY/1200 1650–1805, courtesy of Chris Willmore, Yate town council; TNA, E 164/39.
46   Cornwall RO, CY/1202, 1203, 1205, 1207, 1208, and 1209.

in an extant account book.[47] In 1771 the 'constituted farm of Belsires', *c.*153 a., was divided into two, 'Higher' or Millards farm, and 'Lower' or Poolhouse Farm, and they continued to be worked into the 19th century.[48] Between 1650 and *c.*1830 Yate manor had halved in size.[49]

A survey made during Dennis Gawden's lordship in 1659 outlined the structure of the manor: the total acreage (excluding 74 a. woodland) was 3,447 a., comprising 1,996 a. demesne and copyholds, *c.*832 a. freeholds and roads, and *c.*618 a. common. The 44 tenements included *c.*241 a. of demesne lands, then known as 'Blagden's Court' or 'Blagden's tenement' after the family in occupation.[50] This survey also illustrates the destruction of the deer parks. In 1614 Bassett leased the court and demesne to John Crowther of Iron Acton, who subsequently sold his lease to John Blagden. Crowther's lease entitled him to clear all the trees and underwood from the 'Two Parks, Kitchen Close, the Conygre, the Moore Meade, and the Pye Meade for the amending and bettering of the said grounds', and allowed him to sell the timber without reimbursing Bassett.[51] By 1659 the two parks were referred to as Hither Park Leys and Farther Park Leys, suggesting that by then their clearance and transition to agricultural land was complete.[52]

Tenement size varied from 2 a. to 146 a. Occupants, some with multiple holdings, were mostly dairy farmers, although many also kept sheep, pigs and poultry. Many still held arable in the open fields: Northfield and Westfield (north and west of Goose Green), Upfield (east of Church Lane), and Duckmead (immediately south of Station Road); and there were also orchards and a tanhouse on the manor.[53] But the process of selling and reconstituting tenements after 1677 encouraged the inclosure of the open fields by private agreement,[54] so that by 1844 only the parish commons and wastes remained to be inclosed by act of parliament.[55]

These common lands retained significance to Yate's economy well into the 18th century. From Stanshawes to the western parish edge in the south, north along the boundary with Iron Acton and Rangeworthy, and over Mapleridge common in the north-east, they comprised *c.*600 a.[56] Cottages were built on the ancient heath in the west; and more generally the commons provided fuel and pasture for cattle. When the Caters, lords of Yate manor, attempted to prosecute several parish farmers for trespass and illegally cutting wood, the farmers retaliated in 1745 with a formal defence of their common rights, claiming that they had retained both 'common of pasture for all manner of Cattle and common of estovers [the right to take wood]' when Beckford had released their lands from the manor in the 1670s.[57]

47   Bodl. Lib. MS. Top. Glouc. f. 3.
48   Cornwall RO: CY 1609–1610; see pp. 45, 47–8.
49   GA, D 1610/E 120; GDR, T 1/207.
50   GA, D 1610/E 120; see p. 29.
51   GA, D 1086/T87.
52   GA, D 1610/E 120.
53   GA, D 1610/E 120; GDR inventories, 1622–1699 *passim*; GDR, T 1/207.
54   GA, D 1923, bundle 17.
55   GA, Q/RI/164.
56   Taylor, *Map of Glos.* (1777); Greenwood, *Map of Glos.* (1824); OS Map 1", sheet 35 (1830 edn).
57   GA, D 2772, defence of common rights Yate, 1745; D 1923.

Brinsham manor, like Yate, had by 1700 become a large farming estate with no resident lord, though its history was less turbulent.[58] A detailed survey of c.1700 recorded, apart from the demesne of 248 a., 11 tenements totalling approximately 109 a., with individual holdings ranging from 35 a. to below 1 a. This was one more holding than a decade earlier, but by 1767 there were 15, and the remaining demesne had been divided into two tenements, of 53 a. and 161 a.[59] Pastoral farming predominated; in 1767 Brinsham manor comprised 157 a. pasture, 131 a. meadow, 13 a. woodland and only 3 a. arable.[60]

Evidence from Yate probate inventories indicates that dairy farming prevailed through the 18th century. Although fewer sheep are recorded among the estates, the majority continued to keep pigs and cattle, producing cheese and preserving bacon.[61] Two farming estates included brewhouses, while others had maltmills and produced beer and cider.[62]

Trades and Mineral Extraction

In 1608 there were 15 weavers, five clothiers and two tailors, as well as two miners included among the able bodied men of Yate.

Table 2 *Occupations in Yate 1608*[63]

Gentleman	3	Tailor	2
Servant	6	Labourer	8
Clothier	5	Carpenter	3
Yeoman	4	Clerk (Rector)	1
Husbandman	29	Miner	2
Weaver	15	Shoemaker	1
Smith	3	Tanner	1

Weaving, as an adjunct to sheep husbandry and farm labour generally, occupied parishioners from before 1600 until c.1650.[64] Two Yate weavers, Thomas Hiett and Maurice Neale, tenanted and probably also worked pastureland on Brinsham manor c.1605;[65] and some farmhouse attic windows, such as Hall End, were enlarged to improve light for weaving.[66] Few references to weaving in Yate are found after 1650, reflecting a general decline in the south Gloucestershire textile industry.[67] The feltmaking and millinery trades, specialities of neighbouring Rangeworthy, Westerleigh and Frampton Cotterell, also employed Yate inhabitants, c.1780–c.1850.[68]

58 See pp. 31–3.
59 GA, D 674a/E2, E40, P1.
60 GA, D 674a/E40.
61 GDR inventories, 1701–c.1740, *passim*.
62 GDR inventories, 1716 x2, 1732; also 1681 and 1699.
63 Smith, *Men and Armour*, 215–17.
64 GDR wills, 1576/36.
65 GDR wills, 1602/123; 1609/99; GA, D 674a/M30.
66 Site visit, 2012.
67 R. Perry, 'Glos. woollen industry', *Trans. BGAS*, 66 (1945), 49–137 (97–8).
68 GDR wills, 1789/6, 1817/54, 1843/43; GA, Q/Gc5/1–3; *Children's Employment Commission, 1st Report. Mines*, pt. II (Parl. Papers 1842 [C. 381] xvi), 31–46; J.S. Moore, *Goods and Chattels of our Forefathers* (1976); L.J. Hall, *Rural Houses of North Avon and South Glos. 1400–1720* (1983), 99.

Coal was mined on a small scale from 1584 or earlier, and two miners lived in Yate in 1608.[69] Thereafter the economic importance grew of coal deposits in the west and centre of the parish, and limestone quarried from its eastern ridge.[70] By 1638 Yate manor conveyances recorded stone quarries and limekilns, and potential, if not actual, 'cole pitts' and 'cole mynes'.[71]

Purchasers were entitled to excavate their land, and so to derive additional income, although the lord as owner of subsurface minerals took a fee.[72] Richard Belsire, who let Upper (later Millards) farm in 1708, for £1 7s. annually, demanded an additional £6 13s. 4d. for coal works established on the land. Later leases of Poolhouse (which became part of Yate Colliery works in the 19th century)[73] and Millards farms reserved to Belsire the right to work coal and limestone.[74] Before 1750 Thomas Chester, lord of Brinsham manor, agreed to lease for 31 years an 18 a. allotment, the Hollys or Holly Bushes, in the west of the parish, to Henry Creswicke and Gabriel Wayne, who worked coal in various parishes around Bristol;[75] the rent was 2s. 6d. for every £1 of coal raised.[76] Robert Stokes of Stanshawes (d. 1723), instructed in his will that the limekiln and coalmines 'about' the manor be let to support his widow.[77]

The parish poor also benefited. In 1779 the expediency of inclosing Yate's commons was questioned, 'as it would incapacitate many poor families from pursuing their present business, who now employ themselves in carrying coal from the pits to sell round the country, and depasture their horses on these commons.'[78] Coal's importance continued into the 19th century, when larger enterprises, then styled collieries, were established and the railway introduced.[79]

Agriculture and Industrialisation from c.1800

Yate remained a predominantly agricultural parish until the 1920s. Pastoral farming continued alongside, and often in conjunction with the growing extractive industries.

Agriculture c.1800–c.1950

Beside the Randolphs at Yate and Brinsham, and the Stokes of Stanshawes,[80] there were five other significant landholders in the parish in 1842: in the east above Mapleridge common George Bengough held Hall End farm (formerly 'Foords') and Shortwood (242 a. total). Frederick Ricketts held 162 a. immediately north of these, including the second Hall End farm (formerly 'Baynhams'). In the west Samuel Long and the Alway family held adjacent estates of 144 a. and 102 a. Sir Christopher Codrington of Dodington's two

69   See pp. 47–50.
70   See pp. 50–1.
71   GA, D 1923, bundle 13; D 1610/E 120.
72   Cornwall RO, CY/1200; GA, D 1923.
73   Below, p. 47.
74   Cornwall RO, CY/1207, CY/3788, CY/3790.
75   GA, D 2957/356/1; D 2957/146/159.
76   GA, D 2957/356/1.
77   *Wilts. N&Q*, VI (1908–10), 50.
78   Rudder, *Glos.* 854.
79   See pp. 8–10.
80   See Manors and Estates chapter.

Yate holdings totalled 175 a. No other farms exceeded 75 a. Of the larger owners only John, Thomas and William Alway worked their own lands, and tenants occupied almost 90 per cent of Yate's farmland.[81]

Henry de Beaumont Randolph sold Yate and Brinsham manors (c.1,000 a.) in 50 lots in 1911–12, including Court farm (255 a.) and 10 smaller farms and smallholdings, 24 lots of pasture land, and 12 houses and cottages.[82] Likewise Stanshawes manor was broken up, c.1920, into two farms and the Court as a private residence.[83]

In 1869–70 18 principal farms were recorded in Yate; the 1909 valuation named 28.[84] In 1926 37 of 64 farm holdings were under 20 a., and only 11 over 100 a. By 1956 the overall number had increased slightly to 66.[85]

Arable land in 1801 included 64 a. wheat, 14½ a. barley, 30 a. oats, and 32½ a. pulses and potatoes.[86] The total, 141 a., was substantially less than in 1842, when 267 a. were cultivated in a three-course rotation of wheat or barley, oats or potatoes, and clover; but far more land, 2,447 a., was pasture.[87] After 600 a. of common land were inclosed by act of parliament in 1844,[88] cultivation increased, so that by 1866 the arable acreage exceeded 560 a., with 1,681 a. reserved for permanent pasture.[89]

Table 3 *Parish agricultural returns for Yate 1866–1956*[90]

Year	Wheat (acres)	Barley (acres)	Oats (acres)	Cattle	Cattle for Dairy	Sheep	Pigs
1866	564.75	82	78.25	843	288	888	580
1896	182	57.5	85	927	353	432	495
1926	81	7	57	906	319	386	282
1956	106.25	19.25	51	1374	504	661	766

Thereafter wheat cultivation declined until c.1950, while cattle, sheep and pig numbers increased, although available pasture land, c.1,300–1,400 a. in 1900, scarcely changed.[91] From 1926 substantial numbers of poultry were also kept.[92] Despite the clear dairying bias, most Yate farms surveyed in 1943 worked both arable and pasture; wartime attempts to increase domestic production may have stimulated the increase in arable acreage recorded in 1956.[93]

81   GDR, T 1/207; YHC, D/2734 M. Isaac, *Farms of Yate* (c.2004), 9–10.
82   YHC, Sale Particulars 1911.
83   See p. 36.
84   OS *Reference Book* 1869–70.
85   TNA, MAF 68/3295; MAF 68/4533.
86   *1801 Crop Returns Eng.*
87   TNA, IR 18/2952.
88   GA, Q/RI/164.
89   TNA, MAF 68/25 (1866).
90   TNA, MAF 68/25 (1866); 68/1609 (1896); 68/3295 (1926); 68/4533 (1956).
91   Ibid.
92   TNA, MAF 68/3295 (1926); 68/4533 (1956).
93   TNA, MAF 68/4533 (1956); MAF 73/14/69.

Occupational Structure

Nineteenth-century occupational structure reflected Yate's agricultural character. In 1831, when no-one was recorded as engaged in manufacture, 101 of the 824 inhabitants were farm labourers; 24 farmers employed additional hands, but 12 worked their lands alone. A further 28 were retail or handicrafts workers, and 23 were described simply as labourers.[94] Although by 1881 the population had risen to 1,255 in the wake of railway and mining activities, and the range of occupations had diversified, farming remained the largest occupation; there were 103 agricultural labourers, 66 workers in extractive industries, and only 13 in communications and transport.[95] By 1900 several Yate farmers also engaged in mineral extraction, digging shallow celestine deposits on their land, and limestone for burning.[96] Farm work saw a decline only when factory manufacture was introduced from *c.*1920, to 74 men and women on Yate's farms in 1926, and 61 in 1956.[97]

Coal Mining

Incorporated mining operations were attempted in 1790 when James Tillie's widow Mary let land on Poolhouse farm (formerly part of the Belsire estate)[98] to Thomas Brooke of Sodbury and others, joint proprietors 'in a coal work in the parish'. The lease allowed them to sink pits and erect buildings and engines on the land, and included detailed restrictions on the proper drainage, fencing and in-filling of pits; it also stipulated a weekly royalty of 2s. for every £1-worth of coal extracted.[99] When the lease expired the coal works were let to Robert Ritherdon of London, who was required to pay additional rents to cover the 'coal rents' due from Tillie to Yate's manorial lord.[100] Throughout this period the land continued as a dairy farm, occupied and worked by William Ludlow, who also had Millards farm immediately north of the Poolhouse estate. Although both farms were offered for sale by auction in 1810, Ludlow continued as Tillie's tenant until at least 1819.[101]

'Considerable coal works' were reported in Yate in 1803.[102] By 1824 coal pits were mapped north of Poolhouse farm and across the 'ancient heath' (also 'Yate Lower Common', 'Cock Shute Common' and 'Engine Common').[103] By 1830 the workings in the west of the parish were collectively marked as Yate Colliery.[104] In 1841 the firm of Staley & Parker worked two pits on Yate Common, and Long & Co. three.[105]

The Bristol and Gloucester Railway, extended from Coalpit Heath to Gloucester in 1844, provided the infrastructure necessary for Yate to supply Bristol's increasing demand for coal. Unsurprisingly, there was no evident local resistance, since the route through the parish directly served the collieries, either by running through the coal

94   *Census,* 1831.
95   *Census,* 1881.
96   *Kelly's Dir. Glos.* (1897 edn), 367–8; see below.
97   TNA, MAF 68/3295 (1926); 68/4533 (1956).
98   See p. 43.
99   Cornwall RO, CY/3786.
100 Cornwall RO, CY/3787.
101 Cornwall RO, CY/3785, 3790, 3788, 3789.
102 Rudge, *Hist. of Glos.* II, 367.
103 Greenwood, *Map of Glos.* (1824); GDR, T 1/207.
104 OS Map 1", sheet 35 (1830 edn).
105 *Children's Employment Commission, 1st Report. Mines,* pt. II, 31–46.

workings, or by traversing the lands of the colliery proprietors or the owners of mineral rights. Eventually the line served Yate Colliery via sidings to the mainline.[106]

Yate Colliery

Samuel Long, from a family of wealthy clothiers at Charfield and Wotton-under-Edge, probably came to Yate during the 1830s. In 1838 he owned the Poolhouse farm estate, then occupied by Jonathan Corbett Neale,[107] and he remained proprietor of Yate colliery until his death in 1845. His sons Samuel, Paul and Nathaniel, and latterly Nathaniel's widow Sarah, continued his interests in Yate coal until 1878.[108] In 1826 Samuel (the elder) and his partner Christopher Keeling, a Cromhall miner, had leased from Thomas, Lord Ducie, rights to work coal on Cromhall common.[109] Long & Co. encompassed several such partnerships, trading initially as Long, Keeling and Nowell with William Nowell of Wickwar, and then his widow after 1856. Keeling appears to have left the partnership before 1861.[110] By 1845 the colliery manager was Handel Cossham, later an established mineowner in the Bristol coalfield, city MP and mayor of Bath.[111]

Long & Co. leased mineral rights to Engine Common, the Poolhouse farm estate, part of Eggshill Common south of Station Road, and the commons in Iron Acton adjoining Yate's eastern boundary. Walter Long of Rood Ashton (in Steeple Ashton, Wilts.) owned the mineral rights in Iron Acton as manorial lord. This unrelated Long family were wealthy Trowbridge clothiers whose forebears had purchased Iron Acton manor c.1711.[112] Walter's son, Richard Penruddocke Long, and grandson, Walter Hume Long, continued to let the mineral rights to Long & Co. after the manor was sold in 1881. They also let rights to Engine Common workings to Randolphs of Yate, and claimed annual dead (fixed) rents as well as royalties on coal raised.[113]

At one of Staley & Parker's pits the shaft was 45 fathoms (82 m) deep, and a 60 hp. steam pumping engine was employed to keep the mine dry, although in summer it generally only operated 3–4 days per week. The deeper shafts at Long's works, some 60 fathoms (110 m), required more regular pumping, and operated a 40 hp steam engine for three hours daily.[114]

By mid-century Long & Co., then sole proprietors of Yate Colliery, raised household and steam coal from two pits. No. 1, or 'Old Pit', lay immediately north of Broad Lane and east of the railway line, to which it was connected by a branch. No. 2, 'New Pit', was on Engine Common, midway along the boundary with Iron Acton.[115] From c.1855 the company also had a bank of 12 limekilns (purported to be the longest in England)

106 GA, Q/Rum/151 and 156; see p. 10.

107 GDR, T 1/207.

108 WSA, 515/36, 39, 45; *Slater's Dir. Glos.* (1852 edn), 154; *Bristol Mercury*, 15 Feb. 1862; D. Hardwick, 'A Long Story', *Glos. Society for Industrial Archaeology Journal* (2002), 46–54.

109 GA, D 654/II/16/B1; Hardwick, 'A Long Story'.

110 *Bristol Mercury*, 1846 and 1862; *Post Office Dir. Glos.* (1856 edn), 394.

111 *ODNB*, s.a. Cossham, Handel (1824–90), colliery owner and politician (accessed 19 Feb. 2015).

112 Rudder, *Glos.* 214; Hardwick, 'A Long Story'; WSA, 947/925.

113 W. Chitty, *Historical Account of the Family of Long* (1889), 24; WSA, 515/36–49.

114 *Children's Employment Commission, 1st Report. Mines*, pt. II, 31–46.

115 WSA, 515/45; see p. 10.

connected to Barnhill quarry via a tramway. These burnt local limestone and were
fuelled by the inferior and waste coals. In 1877 the company estimated that they could
produce on average 200–240 tons of lime a week.[116]

Table 4 *Yield from Yate Colliery 1872–86*[117]

Year	Tons raised (over 6 month periods)
1872	8,770
1874	3,592
1876	3,790
1878	5,768
1883	3,375
1885	5,241
1886	6,216

In six months during 1872 Old Pit yielded 2,221 tons, and New Pit 6,549 tons. In
spring 1873 the mines were flooded when the Frome burst its banks, resulting in a
considerable decline in production, so that the colliery works had to be improved. Sarah
Long, by then widowed, left the company in 1878, which became public, and sought
investment to fund the necessary alterations. In 1882 additional funds were raised by
mortgaging the colliery, but yield declined further the following year when installation
of a new pumping engine disrupted operations. Despite colliery improvements, in 1886
the mortgagees refused to finance the necessary completion of the works undertaken.
Thereafter the only coal raised was used to power the pumping engines to keep the
mines dry enough to reopen, should company finances be revived. In spring 1887 the
colliery failed to sell at auction, and Mr F.H. Jones, already associated with the company,
bought the reversion in fee for £1,000. Despite continued attempts to attract investment
and so resume work, the pumping engines stopped permanently in February 1888.[118]

In 1841 Staley & Parker employed up to 35 men including five or six boys under 13.
Because the seam was narrow it was claimed that younger men were needed to work it.
Men over 15 earned 15s.–£1 weekly, and boys 6–9s., for an eight- or nine-hour day. Long
& Co. employed 50 men, but no boys under 12, and the lowest weekly wage was 7s.[119] In
1881 there were 55 miners and colliery employees in the parish, including engine drivers,
firemen and labourers. After the mine closed in 1888 many families left Yate to seek work
in the South Wales coalfields.[120]

Eggshill Colliery

A second colliery, established at the southern limit of Yate on Eggshill (also Yate)
Common, was working before 1887 and continued until *c.*1907, but its development is

116   HER S. Glos. no. 2059; *Post Office Dir. Glos.* (1856 edn), 394; WSA, 515/45.
117   WSA, 515/39, sample from reports 1872–86.
118   WSA, 515/39, 43–9.
119   *Children's Employment Commission, 1st Report. Mines,* pt. II, 31–46.
120   *Census,* 1881; YHC, Yate British School log book, 1888.

poorly documented.[121] It may have occupied the site of much older works, as the remains of an old pump recorded in the shaft in 1887 were made of hollowed-out oak timber supposed to predate 1712.[122]

From 1897 clay raised from the shaft was used by the Yate Fireclay and Brick Co. Ltd to produce firebricks. Their partially mechanized works stood next to the coalmine; the clay was ground down and dampened, and moulded by hand before firing in kilns.[123] The colliery closed when the company was dissolved in 1910, bringing coalmining in Yate to an end.[124] The site was purchased by Wickwar Chemical Company before 1911, and was known as Yate Chemical Works by 1924.[125]

Limestone Quarries

Like coal, limestone extraction was well established in Yate, but until the 19th century was worked on a relatively small scale. The collieries stimulated Barnhill Quarry to produce more stone for lime production.[126] An 1886 map depicts quarries along the length of the limestone ridge on the eastern parish boundary, at Yate Rocks, and to the east of Yate Court.[127] Worked by local men, the quarries also supported masons, stone-cutters and carriers.[128] A quarrying company was established in neighbouring Chipping Sodbury by 1876.[129] By 1909 John Arnold and Sons owned Barnhill Quarry, signalling the beginning of incorporated works in Yate.[130] In 1928 Arnold and Sons became part of British Quarries Ltd. which between *c.*1933 and 1943 gained control of most Yate stone quarries by purchasing land and farms.[131] Before 1943 it owned several former manorial farms, including Oxwick, Brinsham and Tanhouse, which it leased as working concerns, allowing dairy farming to continue alongside stone extraction.[132]

Amalgamated Roadstone Corporation (ARC) in 1946 acquired British Quarries.[133] Works were concentrated along the limestone ridge between Yate and Chipping Sodbury. Barnhill Quarry covered *c.*152 a. south of Love Lane, with its sister quarry, 'Southfields', also owned by ARC, north of the road. In 1968 these quarries together produced *c.*750,000 tons of limestone. The stone quarried was used as road metal, agricultural lime, and aggregate for pre-mixed concrete. Most of the quarries' output was used for roadstone, and used in building local motorways, including the M4. Processing required

121 *Proc. CNFC*, 9 (1890), 178; HER S. Glos. no. 18384–5; YHC, surveyor's letter, *c.*1985; OS Map 6", Glos. LXIX.SW (1903 edn); *Kelly's Dir. Glos.* (1906 edn), 371–2.
122 *Proc. CNFC*, 9 (1890), 178.
123 *Kelly's Dir. Glos.* (1897 edn), 367–8; L. Richardson and R.J. Webb, 'Brickearths, Pottery and Brickmaking in Glos.', *Proc. Cheltenham Nat. Sciences Soc.*, I. no. 5 (1911), 315–19; HER S. Glos. no. 18385.
124 *London Gazette*, 28338, p.1057.
125 Richardson and Webb, 'Brickearths, Pottery and Brickmaking.'; OS Map 6", Glos. LXIX.SW (1924 edn).
126 See pp. 48–9.
127 OS Map 6", Glos. LXIX.NW (1886 edn).
128 *Census*, 1881; *Slater's Dir. Glos.* (1852 edn), 154; *Post Office Dir. Glos.* (1856 edn), 394; *Kelly's Dir. Glos.* (1863–97 edns).
129 YHC, H. Lane, Quarries 1.
130 GA, D/2428/1/86 sig. hereditament nos. 12 and 13.
131 YHC, Invoice, corporate papers 1933; H. Lane, Quarries 1.
132 TNA, MAF 73/14/69; M. Isaac, *Farms of Yate*; see p. 46.
133 GA, DA 33 132/1/11; YHC, YHC, D/930/B, H. Lane, Quarries 1.

significant crushing, screening and grading plants on site. ARC had 219 employees in 1968 and was considered the 'largest producing unit in the area'.[134]

In 1972, following a merger, ARC became Amey Roadstone Corporation, but by then Barnhill quarry was closed.[135] By 1967 the quarry was listed as a Site of Special Scientific Interest, recognising the geological importance of its Carboniferous limestone.[136] Although after 1988 the limestone ridge and quarries lay outside Yate's boundaries, quarrying continued in the area. In 2015 Hanson Aggregates produced roadstone and aggregates at their works based at the Ridge (in Chipping Sodbury).[137]

Celestine Extraction

Deposits of the crystalline mineral strontium sulphate or celestine (otherwise spar or strontia) were identified in the Yate area by 1799.[138] It lay in irregular beds, between one and 30 feet below the surface. Significant as the only commercial source of strontium compounds (or 'salts'), used in sugar-refining, pyrotechnics and, more recently, the production of electrical components, it became a unique feature of the parish's economic development.[139] Small-scale manual extraction had begun in Yate by the 1880s, and by 1900 the lords of Stanshawes and Yate manors, and other local landowners, were retrieving or receiving royalties for easily accessible deposits of spar from their lands.[140] By 1909 Charles Matcham of Raysfield had established a commercial outlet for the mineral in Yate, trading as a strontia merchant.[141]

In 1912 C. Pauli, a Bristol sugar broker, with other local speculators including Howes and Young (cattle-market proprietors and local land agents), formed the Bristol Mineral and Land Company. It sought to capitalise on celestine use in German beet sugar refineries by stimulating a reciprocal trade in refined sugar. Its intervention rationalised celestine production in Yate and, although exports to Germany ceased during wartime, the company continued to oversee the extractive works in Yate until the 1990s. After 1941 it was a subsidiary of the British chemical concern, Albright and Wilson Ltd.[142]

From its inception, Bristol Mineral and Land, and board members, bought up tracts of land in Yate, including substantial parts of the former manorial estates.[143] By 1918 its workings extended over five miles, from Cromhall in the north-west to its headquarters at Stanshawes Court in the south. A series of pits was dug in fields east of the court

134 YHC, D/296, written statement to accompany Yate and CS Town Map 1967; YHC, D/948; GA, DA 33 132/1/11.

135 YHC, D/886/8.

136 Avon CC, *Survey of Mineral Working in Avon: Report of Survey* (1978), 114.

137 Site visit, 2012; South Glos. Council, Permitted Sites Oct. 2012.

138 G.S. Gibbs, 'Discovery of sulphate of Strontia, near Sodbury, Glos.' *Journal of Natural Philosophy, Chemistry and the Arts*, II (1799), 535–6.

139 YHC, *Memoirs of the Geological Survey on the Mineral resources of Great Britain*, II (2nd edn 1918), 48–9; 'Celestine Production', *Mine and Quarry Engineering* (Sept. 1960), 363; Avon CC, *Survey of Mineral Working*, 51; S. Glos. Mines Research Group, H. Lane and D. Hardwick, *Celestine – One of the Old Mineral Industries of Yate* (2013), 7.

140 YHC, copy report of the Strontia and Spar Committee, Nov. 1902.

141 GA, D2428/1/86 (Yate) D2428/1/25 (Cromhall).

142 YHC, R.E Threfall, *Story of a Hundred Years of Phosphorus Making, 1851–1951* (1951); *Mine and Quarry Engineering* (Sept. 1960); Avon CC, *Survey of Mineral Working*.

143 See p. 37; GA, D 6822/70 sale particulars 1911; YHC, Yate House Estate sale particulars 1911; and sales 1944; TNA, MAF 73/14/69; Threfall, *Story of a Hundred Years*.

Figure 11 a & b *Celestine excavation in north Yate, c.1980 (photographs courtesy of A. & H. Lane).*

known as Big Christopher, Little Christopher and Wickham Hill; other groupings of pits lay around Goose Green and Brickhouse farm in the village centre, following the road north to Tanhouse Lane.[144] Once the ground had been exhausted it was filled in and sold. The progress of extraction directly influenced the pattern of post-war urban development; sales in 1944 of worked sites at the centre of Yate were advertised as suitable for commercial construction. In 1951 government-supported restrictions prevented building on sites not yet worked for celestine, and infilling prior to further excavation was regulated by the Planning Commission. This ensured that agricultural production and urban development could continue without disruption.[145]

At first the company extracted the mineral by hand. The spar was transported to Yate Station, then by rail to Avonmouth docks.[146] Mechanised excavation began in 1947, and from 1959 Frederick Parker Ltd of Leicestershire opened a treatment plant in Yate to crush, clean and grade the celestine before transportation.[147] Before the company formalized operations, numerous diggers and cleaners were employed *ad hoc*. Wages, and therefore productivity, varied greatly, with uneven payment made by the day, yard or ton.[148] In 1960 the company's labour force totalled 24, of whom 11 were quarrymen, and the remainder plant workers, drivers, maintenance and office personnel.[149] In 1978 the workforce remained similar: 18 on extraction and processing, four on transport, and five on administration.[150]

In 1915 celestine fetched between 10s. and 11s. per ton at Yate quarry. From 1960 Yate was producing 90 per cent of the world's celestine, some 7,000 tons annually, of which most was exported to the United States.[151] Production stopped temporarily in 1970, but the Yate works re-opened in 1975 and continued operations on a more modest scale until 1995; extraction ceased at this point as the company struggled to compete with more economical, international producers, and due to the parish's celestine beds having been exhausted.[152]

Local Amenities

Yate's industries expanded during the 19th century, while agriculture continued to dominate, but there was a corresponding growth in commerce and amenities. An inn was recorded in 1686, and others followed from the 1850s.[153] A fortnightly market was held at the Railway Hotel in 1889 and later.[154] Described in 1903 as a regular livestock market, it continued until c.1986.[155] Local businesses proliferated along Station Road, the

---

144 YHC, *Memoirs of the Geological Survey.*
145 GA, D 4881/5; YHC, *Mine and Quarry Engineering* (Sept. 1960); Avon CC, *Survey of Mineral Working;* see p. 57.
146 YHC, *Memoirs of the Geological Survey; Mine and Quarry Engineering* (Sept. 1960).
147 YHC, *Mine and Quarry Engineering* (Sept. 1960).
148 YHC, copy report of the Strontia and Spar Committee, Nov. 1902.
149 YHC, *Mine and Quarry Engineering* (Sept. 1960), 370.
150 Avon CC, *Survey of Mineral Working,* 49.
151 YHC, *Memoirs of the Geological Survey; Mine and Quarry Engineering* (Sept. 1960).
152 Avon CC, *Survey of Mineral Working;* S. Glos. Mines Research Group, H. Lane and D. Hardwick, *Celestine – One of the Old Mineral Industries of Yate* (2013), 23.
153 See p. 84.
154 *Kelly's Dir. Glos.* (1889 and later edns).
155 Ibid. OS Maps 6", Glos. LXIX.NW, SW (1903 edns); M. Isaac, *Farms of Yate.*

Figure 12 *The Railway Hotel, established on Station Road by 1856 (photographed c.1910).*

main thoroughfare through the parish. By 1914 Yate had merchants dealing in coal and celestine; there were several grocers, bakers and outfitters as well as a post office and a Bank of England branch.[156]

Modern Industry and the New Town Development

Factory Production

The First World War significantly altered Yate's economic structure, since its transport infrastructure and available space made the area particularly suitable for factory development.[157] McAlpine Government Contracting Co. bought part of the extensive former colliery site north of Station Road; and from *c.*1916 prisoners of war encamped next to Westerleigh Road helped to construct an aerodrome and aircraft repair depot for the Royal Flying Corps, whose base was south of Station Road. The airfield lay between Yate Junction and Poole Court, which served as the officers' mess.[158]

After military use ceased at the end of the war, the airfield site was taken over in 1925 by George Parnall & Co. This was an offshoot of a Bristol shopfitting company, which during the First World War had contracted to manufacture and recondition naval aeroplanes. After the war George Parnall left the firm, which had returned to its former trade, to pursue aircraft development, and established his own company at

156 *Kelly's Dir. Glos.* (1914 edn).
157 See pp. 6–10.
158 OS Maps 6", Glos. LXIX.NW, SW (1926 edns); YHC, report of Swiss Legation on Prisoner of War camp at Yate, May 1917; YHC, D/29.

Figure 13 *Yate's first factory: the Parnall works, c.1945.*

Yate.[159] Take-up of the company's plans was poor and it sold the east end of the site to Newman Electrical Motors in 1932.[160] In 1935 George Parnall & Co. was sold to Nash and Thompson Ltd, and Parnall Aircraft Ltd., a new public company, was constituted.[161]

In 1935 Parnall's site extended over 142 a., and included five large flight and construction sheds, a power plant, workshops and stores accommodating a lacquering shop, wood, metalwork and fitting shops. During the Second World War the site produced machine-gun turrets and undertook aircraft assembly for the RAF; although the last plane to bear the Parnall name was a prototype developed in 1938. Aircraft assembled on site between *c*.1939 and 1941 included the Armstrong Whitworth 'Whitley'

159 YHC, D/29; YHC, Parnall Aircraft Ltd prospectus 1935; S. Gillett, 'The Aircraft Industry in Avon and South Glos.' (1999) MSc thesis, Ironbridge Institute (copy in GA).
160 OS Map 25", Glos. LXIX.5 (1921 edn); HER S. Glos. no. 8899; YHC, Newmans Industries Training Brochure *c*.1960; Gillett, thesis, 74.
161 Gillett, thesis, 74.

bomber.[162] Parnall's neighbour, by 1936 trading as Newman Industries Ltd., was based at the eastern depot on the site and at Poole Court; it produced artillery during the war.[163]

Despite Parnall's confidence that they were 'out of the danger zone', the Yate factories were targeted by the Luftwaffe from the outbreak of war.[164] Air raids in February and March 1941 destroyed much of the factory site and killed 55 employees. Parnall's factory was rebuilt by 1944 but ceased aircraft manufacture in 1945.[165] After a merger in 1958 with the Radiation Group, production of Jackson electrical cookers was transferred to Yate in 1961. By the 1970s the company produced a range of appliances and electrical components for T.I. Jackson Ltd (Creda), and in 2006 Indesit began production on the Parnall's site, which it continued to occupy in 2014.[166]

After 1945 Newman Industries continued to manufacture industrial and fractional electrical motors for domestic use and in mining and textiles. By 1970 sales exceeded £7 million, half of which were made abroad. In 1988 Newman's left Yate and the site was cleared for new housing and retail development.[167]

By the 1950s these factories were Yate's most significant employers. Parnall's workforce, drawn from Yate and the Bristol area, rose from c.200 in 1920 to 1,500 in 1970. Newman's had c.2,000 employees in 1965.[168] The companies played an important social role, providing housing and recreational facilities for their workers, and education and training programmes in a range of technical occupations. The influx of new families into Yate, drawn by the factories, directly influenced the development of the new town.[169]

Industry and the New Town

As population increased, county and district planners sought to restrict industrial and commercial activity within the town in favour of housing. In 1964 industry in Yate, reckoned then to employ 3,200 people,[170] was limited to specific areas, and in 1968 existing industrial enterprises flanking Station Road were considered an 'inhibiting factor' in developing the new town's commercial centre. Consequently further industrial development in the centre was prevented, and existing businesses were encouraged to move to prescribed areas.[171]

Industry was henceforth concentrated to the north-west of the urban area, between the railway line and Yate parish boundary.[172] This area was being developed as the Stover trading estate by 1964, when leases were granted to Avon Rubber, Colgate-Palmolive, E.N. Heath (wallpaper factors) and MacFisheries. Because of the estate's proximity to the

162 YHC, Parnall Aircraft Ltd prospectus, 1935; YHC, photograph of Parnall works with Whitley bomber, c.1945 (*Creda* Archive); Gillett, thesis, 77–8.
163 OS Maps 25", Glos. LXIX.5, 6 (1921 edns); HER S. Glos. no. 8899; YHC, commemorative shell; TNA, HO 192/1406 Newman Industries Ltd.
164 YHC, D/2105/7 Luftwaffe intelligence target document dated Sept. 1939.
165 YHC, D/2427 diary 1941; memorial in church; site visit, 2012; Gillett, thesis.
166 YHC, *Gazette*, Oct. 1978; Jackson and Creda brochures; local inf.
167 YHC, App 1/54 Newman Industries Training Brochure c.1960; Newman Industries Directors Report Dec. 1970; *Gazette*, Apr 22 1988; F. Walker, *Bristol Region* (1972), 326.
168 YHC, *Gazette*, 22 Apr. 1988; *Glos. Life*, 1970.
169 YHC, App 1/54 Newman Industries Training Brochure c.1960.
170 GA, DA 33 132/1/11.
171 YHC, D/294: Principal Planning Evidence, July 1968.
172 Ibid.

M4 and M5 motorways and the Severn Bridge, these companies used it as a distribution centre.[173] Despite concerns that not enough space was set aside for similar businesses migrating to the area (especially from Bristol, then undergoing redevelopment), it was agreed to increase the estate gradually, rather than outstrip the pace of demand with speculative allocations.[174]

In 2012 Yate's industries remained in the west of the parish. The Badminton and Stover Industrial Estates lay west, and Station Road Estate immediately east, of the railway line. Three business parks had also been developed in the same area.[175]

As urban development progressed concerns were expressed about the quarries in the east of the parish. The spoil heaps at the Ridge were described as 'a serious erosion of the visual amenity' in the direction of Chipping Sodbury, and district planners were reluctant to allow any expansion of the quarries, although they were among Yate's most productive businesses. When the town plans were reviewed in 1968, ARC agreed to remove its plant at Barnhill quarry, then nearing closure, to Southfields, which was still in use.[176] By 1978 some cosmetic landscaping had taken place, in the form of sculpted and planted banks around the site obscuring the works.[177]

ARC's plans to develop the disused quarry as a landfill site faced objections on pollution and traffic congestion grounds, and they were rejected in 1976 and 1984.[178] But after 1990 popular criticism focused on the safety risk posed by the abandoned works, and after two boys were trapped in the site overnight infilling was reconsidered and new security measures implemented.[179] In 2010 160 new homes on the Barnhill site and Chipping Sodbury's first supermarket were proposed; the Waitrose store opened in 2013.

Commercial Development

The focus of commercial development in the new town was Yate's shopping centre, opened in 1965.[180] Situated in the heart of the old village, opposite the White Lion inn and south of the church, it provided space for up to 70 shops. Outlets included food retailers, financial service providers, domestic appliance and furniture shops, and estate agents.[181] An entertainment centre was open by 1970, and a 1980s extension included a large supermarket. Renovations in 1990 enclosed some pedestrian walkways with glass roofs.[182] Besides providing most of the growing new town's shopping amenities, the centre, with ample free parking, hoped to lure Bristol's shoppers out of the city.[183] By 1970, however, the entertainment centre, in particular, was less busy than expected, attributable partly to Yate's demography. Young families of Bristol commuters could not

173 YHC, Stover Trading Estate Development, 1964.
174 YHC, D/294: Principal Planning Evidence, July 1968.
175 South Glos. Council: map of district centres, industrial sites 2012.
176 GA, DA 33 132/1/11; see pp. 50–1.
177 Avon CC, *Survey of Mineral Working.*
178 YHC, D/886/8: *Gazette*, Apr.–Aug. 1976, Sept. 1983–Apr. 1984.
179 YHC, D/886/8: *Gazette*, Nov. 1991; *Bristol Evening Post*, Aug.–Nov. 1996.
180 See pp. 22–3.
181 YHC, D/310 Shopping Centre Brochure *c.*1965; *Glos. Life*, 1970.
182 Yate Shopping Centre Information: http://www.yateshoppingcentre.co.uk/Centre-Information/; *Glos. Life*, 1970; Verey and Brooks, *Glos.* II, 827.
183 *Glos. Life*, 1970.

Figure 14 *Yate Shopping Centre and Newman Industries, c.1965.*

afford to visit the shopping centre complex, and it was not readily accessible from the southern estates without private transport.[184]

Throughout the 1970s Yate's civic amenities were extended around the shopping centre, including a library, emergency services, magistrate's court, leisure and health centres.[185] After 2000 the site was expanded further, adding a new 24-hour supermarket of some 110,000 square feet. In 2013 the shopping centre complex remained the focus of commercial activity in the urban area. Smaller independent shops and businesses continued to trade along the length of Station Road from the west of the parish to its centre.[186]

Although limited by urban growth, some farming continued in the northern half of the ancient parish and at Yate Rocks in the east, but from 1988 much of this area fell outside the re-drawn parish boundaries.[187] Before 2000 dairying in Yate contracted, and

184 *Glos. Life,* 1970.
185 See p. 57.
186 Yate Shopping Centre Information; site visit, 2012.
187 See pp. 65–6.

several farms turned to poultry rearing.[188] Tanhouse Farm, one of the larger former manor farms, diversified its business by offering camping and fishing facilities.[189]

Occupational Structure

In 1965 the main employers within the parish were the manufacturing industries, service and distribution trades, and quarrying. Because two-thirds of the workforce lived elsewhere, it was assumed that many Yate residents worked in Bristol. In 1981 approximately 20 per cent of the town's population worked outside the area, one-third was engaged in manufacture, and only two per cent worked in agriculture.[190] Despite planners' intentions that people should move to Yate to live and work, by 2000 commuting prevailed, especially to Bristol.[191] In 2012 the business and industrial parks west of Yate town, as well as businesses on the periphery of Chipping Sodbury, provided the main areas of employment, mostly in manual labour. Around 12,000 people from Yate and Chipping Sodbury commuted out for work, with 3,500 commuting in.[192]

188 Site visit, Hall End 2012.
189 M. Isaac, *Farms of Yate*; site visit 2012.
190 *Census*, 1981.
191 GA, DA 33 701/3/4, *c.*1965.
192 South Glos. Council, *South Glos. Core Strategy* (2012).

LOCAL GOVERNMENT

Manorial Government

COURTS WERE HELD IN YATE and Brinsham manors from the 14th century or earlier; their apparent decline from the 17th century coincided with non-resident lords, and the manors reforming as farming estates.[1] A court may have been held at Stanshawes, but no evidence of its proceedings has been found.

Yate

Although no records of Yate manorial court survive, there are sporadic references to it. At the inquisition on the death of the lord, John de Willington, in 1338, its pleas and perquisites were worth £1 annually.[2] A court was held in 1410 when William Gore, lord of Brinsham manor, made an order to distrain Thomas Haymond for prosecuting Thomas Neel in the court of Yate over a parcel of land called Welcroft, common to the tenants of both manors.[3] Henry, Lord Daubeney, who held Yate 1509–47, convened a manor court in 1533. Four customary tenants had failed to pay suit to their lord, and were charged with felling trees and clearing lands in the manor for their own use; the matter was pursued in the court of Chancery.[4] Although no specific reference has been found to the court sitting thereafter, when the lords were absentees,[5] tenants in 1624 continued to hold their lands by copy of court roll.[6]

Brinsham

Court rolls for Brinsham manor are extant 1384–1464, draft rolls remain from 1540 and 1554, and a court book covers the period 1605–82.[7] The early courts dealt with admissions to the manor and the transfer of property within it. Fees paid for pannage and the profits from legitimate sales of wood were also received by the court. In 1384 the bailiff, Thomas Neele, was responsible for the sale of wood from the manor, and in 1410 Richard Felawe, a juror 1407–9, was recorded as the 'collector of rents for loping oaks'. The court fined tenants if they failed to pay suit, for 'ruinous' dwellings, for illegally felling trees or fishing without licence, making encroachments or sub-letting parts of customary tenements. Orders of distraint were made for defaulted rents.[8]

1   See Manors and Estates chapter.
2   *Inq. p.m. Glos.* 1302–58, 271–3.
3   GA, D 674a/M27.
4   TNA, C 1/775/3–9, 1533–8.
5   See pp. 32–3.
6   GA, D 1923.
7   GA, D 674a/M27–30.
8   GA, D 674a/M27.

The later courts dealt primarily with tenurial matters. In 1540, in addition to the regulation of tenancies, pannage rights were still paid.[9] Courts convened after 1605 recorded only the entry of new tenants and inheritance of customary tenements, for which a heriot continued to be due.[10]

The Hundred Court of Henbury

Tenants of both manors paid suit to the hundred court convened under the lordship of Ralph Sadleir. A court book remains extant for 1608–19.[11] The court met bi-annually, usually in April and October. 'Yate tithing' was represented by four jurors, primarily copyholders from the manor of Yate, although Thomas Burnell of Brinsham attended until 1611.[12] Presentments and orders from the court largely concerned the regulation of rights of way and watercourses, and the bounds and maintenance of tenements. At the October session, a tithingman and constable were elected and payment of common fine was made, which was maintained at 13s. for the duration of the record.

Parochial Government

Before 1894

The vestry met to administer parish government, presumably from the 16th century, although its meetings are recorded only from 1783. The overseers' accounts, 1782–1822, include notes on vestry proceedings, and separate minute books detailed vestry business 1815–1902.[13]

Two churchwardens served the parish by 1563,[14] and in 1569 they reported that the church lacked a surplice and the windows were in disrepair. These deficiencies may reflect dissatisfaction with liturgical changes imposed during the Elizabethan Reformation.[15] The diocesan court ordered George Buck, who appeared to answer the complaint, to procure a surplice within a month, and to make the requisite repairs.[16] In 1635, 1642 and 1704 the churchwardens were assisted in their duties by two sidesmen.[17]

Richard Dickinson was recorded as parish constable in 1662. Jonathan King held this office in 1664, Robert Tyler in 1715, and Daniel Shipp in 1844.[18]

'Supervisors' of the parish highways were recorded in 1754 when Richard Hill and Robert Cole petitioned quarter sessions to levy a rate of £30 for road repairs. Cole was responsible for collecting rates from Church End, the southern half of the parish, and Hill for Hall End, the northern half.[19] Hill was a gentleman of considerable local and

9   GA, D 674a/M28.
10   GA, D 674a/M30.
11   This para. BRO, AC/M/12/1; also Duke Univ. Lib. Ovsz Box 18 (survey, 1608), f. 3.
12   GA, D 1923.
13   BRO, P St MY/OP/1/a & b; P. St MY/V/1a; YHC, vestry minute books, 1831–1902.
14   GDR vol. 20, p.19.
15   See pp. 97–8.
16   GDR vol. 26, p. 17.
17   GDR, V 5/356T/4–6; GDR vol. 207.
18   TNA, E 179/116/554; ibid. E 179/247/16; GA, Q/SO/4/3; YHC, vestry minute books, 1831–1902.
19   GA, Q/SR/1754.

regional standing, who in 1751 was appointed sheriff for the county.[20] Hall End Farm, a large estate within his jurisdiction as highways supervisor, had been developed by his father (also Richard) as a substantial gentleman's home by *c.*1700.[21]

Apart from Thomas Stokes of Stanshawes in 1784–5, the lords of the three manors were notably absent from the vestry.[22] Likewise the presence of parish clergy was infrequently recorded. Jonathan Hodges, Thomas Tournay's curate, attended annual meetings 1783–5 and 1789; and William Goodenough, rector 1801–42, featured more prominently from 1815.[23] Regular attenders included the principal tenants from Yate and Brinsham manors, occupiers of the larger independent farms, including the Ludlows of Millards and Poolhouse farm, and some parish freeholders.[24] Three generations of the Sturge family, substantial local landowners and Quakers, attended frequently between 1783 and 1831.[25]

In 1823 the vestry commissioned a new meeting room to be built at the north-west corner of the church, and until this opened in *c.*1826 meetings were adjourned to the White Lion inn.[26] The two churchwardens, from 1784 or earlier, were nominated by the vestry;[27] and after 1822 it appointed one for the parish, while the rector selected the other.[28] In 1884 the parish churchwarden was elected by a poll held at the National School.[29]

Until 1836 the vestry was also responsible for nominating overseers of the poor, paying out-relief and maintaining the parish workhouse. An overseer for the 'Church End' of the parish, and one for the 'Hall End', were nominated annually in March, along with two collectors of the parish rates. From at least 1816 three assistant overseers were appointed for each half of the parish.[30]

Women served as both overseers and assistant overseers between 1806 and *c.*1818.[31] Although not electors, maintaining the poor was deemed an appropriate pastoral role for women, but they still had to be property holders to be eligible for local office. All Yate's female overseers were widows or single women with their own estates,[32] and most also had family connections with other vestry members. Anne Pearce and Hannah Ford, assistant overseers for Church End and Hall End in 1817, were succeeded by their sons, Thomas Pearce and Edward Ford;[33] and Ann Whitcomb, also an assistant overseer

20   *London Mag.* Jan. 1751, 44; *Morning Advertiser,* 21–23 Jan 1751.

21   See p. 17.

22   BRO, P St MY/OP/1/a.

23   BRO, P St MY/OP/1/a; P St MY/V/1a; see pp. 91, 99.

24   BRO, P St MY/OP/1/a; P St MY/V/1a; GA, D 674a/E2, P1, E40; D 12430/1/40.

25   BRO, P St MY/OP/1/a; P St MY/V/1a; TNA, PROB 11/1954/204; see pp. 99–100.

26   BRO, P St MY/V/1a.

27   BRO, P St MY/OP/1/a.

28   BRO, P St MY/V/1a.

29   *Western Daily Press,* 1 May 1884, 6.

30   BRO, P St MY/OP/1/a; P. St MY/V/1a.

31   BRO, P St MY/OP/1/a; P. St MY/V/1a.

32   GA wills 1822/110, 1824/96, 1826/94, 1834/220; S. Richardson, 'Petticoat Politicians', *The Historian* 119 (Autumn 2013), 12–15.

33   BRO, P St MY/V/1a; GA, wills 1822/110; 1826/94.

for Hall End in 1817, and proprietor of Hill House, had been preceded by Nathaniel
Whitcomb, the estate holder until his death in 1797.[34]

The departure of women from local office coincided with the Sturges Bourne reforms
of 1818–19, which established select vestries for the maintenance of the poor and made
provision for paid overseers. The select vestry consisted of 'substantial householders',
elected via a weighted voting system based on property holding.[35] Precisely why women
disappeared from parochial politics at Yate is unclear.

A select vestry at Yate was elected in 1820, when a salary of £15 was agreed for
the six overseers nominated for each 'end' of the parish, who held the office in turn.
Householders with a 'Tyburn Ticket' (a certificate exempting them from parochial
duties in reward for securing the conviction of a felon) were allowed a proportion of the
overseer's salary, drawn from the parish poor rate.[36] From 1836 Yate formed part of the
Chipping Sodbury Poor Law Union, served by the union workhouse situated within the
parish.[37] The vestry continued to elect overseers and levy the poor rate until c.1894.[38]

The vestry also appointed a hayward to regulate the use of Yate's commons and
inclosures. In 1821 it ordered the hayward to supervise the demolition of a stable erected
by Richard Werrett on the waste.[39] Daniel Shipp served as hayward in 1844 as well as
constable.[40]

From c.1800 main roads through the parish were administered by the Sodbury
turnpike trust and, after disturnpiking in 1873, the Sodbury highway board.[41] The vestry
retained some involvement; in 1877, at its request, the highway board granted it an
additional way-warden, the better to monitor the state of the parish thoroughfares, which
were increasingly burdened by traffic and the growing population.[42]

From 1894

In 1894 a parish council was elected for Yate, and the Chipping Sodbury Rural District
Council represented the parish at district level.[43] The vestry continued to meet until
at least 1902, but its activities were focused on the maintenance of the church and the
election of churchwardens.[44]

At its inaugural meeting the council agreed to conduct its business in private, but
this decision was overturned by a resolution passed at a meeting of electors in April
1895.[45] Robert Nathaniel Hooper, resident of Stanshawes Court and county councillor for
Chipping Sodbury ward, chaired the meeting, which was also attended by representatives
from the district council.[46]

34   BRO, P St MY/OP/1/a; P. St MY/V/1a; GA, wills 1797/93; 1834/220.
35   BRO, P St MY/V/1a; 58 Geo. III c. 69 & 59 Geo. III c.12; J. Vernon, *Politics and the People* (1993), 19.
36   BRO, P St MY/V/1a.
37   GA, G/SO/8a/1; see pp. 73–5.
38   YHC, vestry minute books, 1831–1902.
39   BRO, P/St MY/V/1a.
40   YHC, vestry minute books, 1831–1902.
41   See pp. 7–8.
42   GA, Q/AH/7/3.
43   YHC, D/730/2; Youngs, *Admin. Units* I, 192.
44   YHC, vestry minute books, 1831–1902.
45   YHC, D/730/2; *Bristol Mercury,* 6 Apr. 1895.
46   *Bristol Mercury,* 6 Apr. 1895.

The parish council was responsible for maintaining recreation grounds in Yate, and monitoring public rights of way. Parish accounts were presented by the assistant overseer. From c.1900 the council also provided checks on the impact of quarrying and spar extraction in the parish, and worked for the extension of utilities and transport links to the settlement. Meetings were held at the National School until 1934, when a new parish hall was built on Station Road.[47]

Robert Nathaniel Hooper of Stanshawes, who regularly chaired parish council meetings, was a justice of the peace for Gloucestershire from 1889, and retained his county council seat in 1901. He was a member of the county education committee in 1903, and of the standing joint committee when he died in 1914.[48] Other prominent Yate residents did not hold parochial office, but were also involved in local and regional government more broadly. Francis Frederick Fox of Yate House was a county magistrate from 1896, and a justice for the Bristol bench, who had been a Bristol alderman 1865–71, and again in 1875. Fox had also been prominent in local associations, notably the Society of Merchant Venturers and the Bristol and Gloucestershire Archaeological Society.[49]

New Town Development and Urban Administration

Yate was represented on Sodbury Rural District Council from its formation in 1935,[50] and the council encouraged residential development to meet the demands of the growing manufacturing community.[51] Responding to Yate's physical and demographic growth, in 1955 the elected membership of the parish council was increased from nine to 11. In 1967 it requested a further increase, and Yate was divided into four wards. The north, west, and central wards each elected four representatives and the south ward three, raising the total number of parish councillors to 15. Each ward was also represented on the district council. A fourth councillor was added to the south ward in 1970, reflecting the growth of residential estates within the ward boundaries.[52]

The progress of urban development created tensions between levels of local government. In 1965 and 1968 district and parish councillors from Yate expressed concern that infrastructure, provision for industrial production, and local amenities were not keeping pace with residential building. Gloucestershire County Council, however, at the public enquiry into the new town development in 1968, considered that no alterations to the existing plans were necessary.[53]

Yate fell within the newly established county of Avon in 1974, in Northavon district.[54] In 1978 the parish council was reconstituted as Yate town council,[55] 'recognising that we

---

47   GA, D 6822/66 (57); Yate town council, Poole Court: parish council minute books, 1894–1970; *Bristol Mercury,* 6 Apr 1895; *Western Daily Press,* 20 Feb. 1899; see pp. 85, 103.
48   *Cheltenham Looker-On,* 2 Mar 1889; *Citizen,* 28 Feb. 1901; *Western Daily Press,* 14 Apr. 1903; *Glouc. J.* 17 Jan. 1914.
49   *Western Daily Press,* 10 Mar. 1875, 17 Oct. 1896, 1 June 1915.
50   Youngs, *Admin. Units* I, 192.
51   *Western Daily Press,* 4 Aug., 6 Sept. 1949.
52   GA, DA/33/185/1.
53   GA, DA 33/701/3/4; DA 33/132/1/11.
54   Youngs, *Admin. Units,* I, 192.
55   Yate town council, Poole Court: parish council minute books, vol. 11.

Figure 15 *Poole Court, c.1910; restored in 1990 as the new town council offices and civic centre.*

have become a truly urban area',[56] and was candid about its purpose: to apply pressure on the district and county councils to deliver on the amenities promised in the town plans, and to concentrate on consolidating a homogeneous society within the urban area through the promotion of community activities and organisations.[57]

When parish boundaries were reviewed in 1980, Sodbury parish council and Yate town council argued that, because of Yate's 'pure urban concept' and Sodbury's 'combined urban and rural roots', two councils were needed to administer the urban area jointly. They rejected proposals for both a single council, and the existing arrangement of four councils (Yate, Sodbury, Dodington and Westerleigh), which had administrative responsibility for parts of the new town that overlapped parish boundaries. It was suggested that the urbanised sections of Dodington and Westerleigh had more in common with the new town and should be transferred to Yate. The town council highlighted its provision of recreational and sports facilities, and the subsidies made to encourage community activities, which had contributed to the formation of a shared identity.[58]

Yate's boundaries were re-drawn in 1988 to encompass the urban area.[59] The boundary with Dodington was re-aligned to the main distributor road to reflect community groupings, and the part of Westerleigh east of the railway line was incorporated into Yate parish as Stanshawes ward.[60] This re-organisation resulted in

56   YHC, D/302/1–2.
57   Ibid. GA, DC 93/6/3–4.
58   GA, P 357a/PC/11/1/2.
59   GA, P 357a/PC/11/1/2; Northavon (Parishes) Order 1988, SI 1988/112; see p. 5.
60   GA, P 357a/PC/11/1/2; Northavon (Parishes) Order 1988, SI 1988/112; OS 1:25 000, sheet 167 (1998 edn).

the removal of Westerleigh (historically Yate) common to Yate. Westerleigh attempted to recoup some of the financial loss the transfer would entail by selling it before the boundary change. The sale was stopped by a court injunction secured by a local campaign, and the common was transferred to Northavon District Council, preserving it as public space.[61] The Local Plan, also issued that year, created a 'breathing space' for development in Yate, limiting urban expansion to allow the new town to mature.[62]

Because of its increased responsibilities Yate town council needed to relocate from a temporary building next to the parish hall to permanent offices. Formerly part of the Newman's complex closed in 1988,[63] Poole Court was restored for use as council offices and a civic centre, opened in 1990.[64] The office of mayor was created in 1993 and was held in conjunction with chairmanship of the council.[65]

Since 1996 Yate has been part of the South Gloucestershire unitary authority, formed from the Northavon and Kingswood districts of the former county of Avon.[66] In 2014 the town council had 17 elected members, representing five wards for the north, central, south, south-east and west of Yate. It continued to support local amenities and advise on the future expansion of the town.[67]

61   GA, P 357a PC 32/1/6; *Gazette*, 18 Mar., 8 Apr. 1988.
62   Yate town council: minutes of the planning sub-committee meeting, 26 June 2012.
63   See pp. 55–6.
64   GA, D 6822/69, Yate town council, Poole Court: parish council minute books, vols. 20 and 23; *Gazette* cuttings, 1988–90.
65   Inf. from Cllr. C. Willmore, Yate town council.
66   Avon (Structural Change) Order 1995, SI 1995/493.
67   http://www.yatetowncouncil.gov.uk (accessed 21 Jan. 2015).

SOCIAL HISTORY

By 1300 Yate manor had a substantial free tenantry. With no resident lord between 1398 and *c.*1700 independent freeholding in the parish increased further, especially when portions of the manor were sold after 1600.[1] Yate's occupational diversity, already apparent in 1608, increased after 1800 with the growth of extractive industries, and then the arrival of the railway.[2] The growing population stimulated school building and other social institutions;[3] and factory-based industries after 1900, with a further increase in population, galvanised plans to develop Yate as a new town from *c.*1959. Although Yate's existing community was intended to provide the nucleus for social expansion, the phasing of construction challenged the development of a homogeneous town identity.[4] The established and new amenities and organisations proved vital to the success of the new town's social life.

Social Structure

Evidence for medieval social structure is most detailed from Yate manor, the largest of the three estates within the parish. The de Willingtons, lords from 1208 to 1398,[5] had settled elsewhere, at Sandhurst,[6] but they were prepared to invest in Yate. In 1218 Ralph de Willington obtained a market grant to be held in his Yate manor, although this was undermined by a rival claim for Sodbury, by William Crassus, made in the same year.[7] John, Ralph's successor, gained a licence to crenellate (fortify) Yate Court and developed the deer park between *c.*1299 and 1302.[8] In 1321 the manor had 38 free tenants, 35 villeins and nine cottagers.[9] In 1327 John de Willington was assessed for tax in Yate with Itchington at 8*s.* 3*d.* The next wealthiest inhabitants, John Bromcroft and Alice de Blakeneye, both free tenants of Yate manor, were assessed for 4*s.* 6¾*d.* and 12*d.* respectively, and at least three other tenants were assessed at 8*d.* each.[10]

When the de Willington male line failed in 1398 a period of absentee lordship at Yate ensued. The Beaumonts of Devon sold the manor to Giles Daubeney in 1501, and in 1504

---

1   See p. 30.
2   Ibid.
3   See pp. 77–8.
4   See pp. 54–60.
5   See pp. 25–9.
6   *VCH Glos.* XIII (forthcoming): Sandhurst.
7   See pp. 41–2.
8   See p. 17.
9   TNA, E 142/24.
10 P. Franklin, *Taxpayers of Medieval Glos* (1993), 89; TNA, E 142/24.

he leased the manor court and demesne to Maurice Berkeley. Although the Berkeleys made substantial alterations to the property, they were not permanent residents.[11] In the military survey of 1522, 62 men were recorded in the parish.[12] With no resident lord, members of other prominent families were reflected in the assessment, including John Neale (assessed at £12), and Alexander Baynham and Thomas Burnell (lord of Brinsham manor) at £10.[13] In 1524–5 Alexander Baynham's goods were valued at £10, and John Neale's at £8. Only Thomas Burnell was valued on lands, worth £10; 16 other residents had goods worth £3 or more, Robert Corbett had goods valued at £2 13s. 4d., and 26 were assessed at £2. The remaining 19 parishioners were assessed on wages of £1–£1 10s.[14]

Both Baynhams and Neales were resident in Yate from 1500 or earlier. John Bennam (also Baynham) was rector of Yate before 1514, and in 1572 Robert Baynham and Thomas Neale were patrons of the benefice, presenting Thomas Baynham to the living.[15] The Baynhams were probably related to a family prominent in the Forest of Dean, and manorial lords in Westbury-on-Severn.[16] Thomas Neale married Elizabeth, whose brother was Alexander Belsire of Yate, a fellow of New College, Oxford.[17] Their son Thomas, was an acclaimed Hebrew scholar and professor of Christ Church, Oxford.[18] He may have been born at Yate Court, c.1519, when his father perhaps lived on the court estate in some fiduciary capacity for the Berkeleys.[19] In 1552 the Baynhams, Neales and Belsires were all substantial tenants on Yate manor. Thomas Belsire held lands worth £2 15s. 7d., Thomas Baynham and Robert Baynham owed rents of £2 19s. and £1 13s. 7d. respectively, and Thomas Neale (on his death, in 1584, a landholder also in Wickwar, Berkeley and Cromhall)[20] held two Yate tenements worth £2 4s. 4d. together.[21] Descendants of the Neales and Belsires continued to hold these tenements after 1600, and became freeholders, c.1650–80.[22]

In 1608 a muster roll recorded no lord of Yate and only two gentlemen, John Crowther, and Christopher Stokes of Stanshawes.[23] Crowther held lands in Iron Acton, and by 1614 had taken on the lease of Yate Court and the demesne of Yate manor.[24] Four other parishioners were listed as yeomen and 29 as husbandmen. A comparable number were engaged in non-agricultural occupations, including five clothiers, 15 weavers and two miners, as well as eight labourers and ten other tradesmen.[25]

---

11   See pp. 28–9.
12   *Military Surv. of Glos, 1522*, 42–3.
13   Ibid.
14   *Bristol and Glos. Lay Subsidy, 1523–27*, 132–4, 301–2.
15   See p. 91.
16   *Visit. Glos. 1623*, 12–16; J. Maclean, 'History of the Manor of Dene Magna', *Trans. BGAS*, 6 (1881–2), 123–209; *VCH Glos. X*, 89.
17   J.A. Neale, *Charters and Records of Neales of Berkeley, Yate and Corsham* (1906) 10; *Alumni Oxon 1500–1714*, II, 1054.
18   MS Bodl. 13 part 1 T. Neale (1566); Neale, *Charters*, 16–18.
19   Neale, *Charters*, 17–18.
20   GDR wills 1585/159.
21   TNA, E 164/39.
22   See pp. 42–3.
23   Smith, *Men and Armour* (1608).
24   GA, D 1086/T87.
25   Smith, *Men and Armour*.

From 1650 Yate's absentee lords sold several tenements to their customary tenants, creating substantial independent estates. The advowson was also granted away to the Baynhams, who between 1600 and 1800 usually presented non-resident clergy.[26] By 1700 Brinsham manor was primarily a farming estate, occupied by tenants of Thomas Chester of Knole Park (Almondsbury).[27]

With no single locus of power in the parish a degree of independence prevailed among its freeholders. Several landowners were nonconformists, who disputed at length with the rectors over paying parish dues.[28] New incoming manorial lords also clashed with more established proprietors. Robert Oxwick, lord of Yate 1679–1740, entered into protracted litigation with the rector, William Mason, regarding the customary payment of tithes in kind.[29] The Caters, who succeeded Oxwick c.1740, attempted to restrict common rights, but those landholders accused of trespass and malicious damage to the woods and commons cited their enduring access rights enshrined before 1700 in their conveyances. A covenant signed by the aggrieved parties resolved to defend their rights and privileges, to protect their own inheritances and the rights of 'all and every other freeholders within the said Manner' who had yet to be challenged.[30]

It was acknowledged before 1800 that the commons provided an important source of subsistence for Yate's poor.[31] Cottages had been erected on the ancient heath in the west of the parish from the medieval period, and some were still occupied into the 19th century.[32] The commons also fostered illicit means of survival. In 1826, 31 members of a gang of thieves, including nine Yate residents, and operating from a cottage on Yate common, were arrested for crimes reputedly perpetrated over a seven-year period.[33]

In 1797 the former manorial estates remained the largest holdings. Beckford Cater, lord of Yate, was assessed for £78 6s., Elizabeth Bromley Chester paid £21 11s. 1d. for Brinsham, and Thomas Stokes £15 8s. 2d. for Stanshawes; all of which were tenanted.[34] Four other assessments exceeded £10. Mary Tillie (also Tilly) paid £26 2s. 11d. for the Belsire estate, an accumulation of tenements sold by Yate manor; a Mr Veale owed £23 4s. 5d. for his farm 'Pinchpoor'; John Codrington owed £12 17s. 1d. for his holdings and Mary Whitcomb paid £10 0s. 11d. for Hill House.[35] In line with the general pattern of Yate landholding, only the last two were owner-occupiers.[36]

The structure of landownership remained stable after 1800, but land use altered markedly. By 1838 the amalgamation of Brinsham and Yate manors concentrated almost one-third of the parish in the hands of Henry Jones Randolph.[37] Six other landowners held more than 100 a. each, including Samuel Long; his was the Tillie (formerly Belsire)

26   See pp. 97–100.
27   See p. 33.
28   See pp. 99–100.
29   See pp. 92–3.
30   GA, D 2772.
31   Rudder, *Glos.* 854.
32   HER S. Glos. no. 14419; GA, Q/RI/164.
33   GA, Q/Gc5/1–3; *Morning Chronicle*, 2 Aug. 1826; *Bath Chronicle*, 10 Aug. 1826.
34   GA, D 12430/1/40.
35   GA, D 12430/1/40.
36   GA, D 12430/1/40.
37   See p. 28.

estate, which would be developed as Yate Colliery. The remaining third of the parish was divided among holdings of 75 a. or smaller. Tenants continued to work most of the land,[38] and in 1842–4 the wastes and commons were inclosed.[39] As Yate's extractive industries expanded from the 1830s, and the Bristol and Gloucester Railway extended through the parish in 1839–44,[40] significant demographic changes occurred.

The population increased sharply from 824 in 1831 to 1,057 in 1841; by 1881 it reached 1,255, having doubled since 1801.[41] In 1831 there were 110 families chiefly employed in agriculture, 27 in trade, manufacture and handicrafts, and 43 unclassified.[42] By 1841, although agriculture remained pre-eminent, 22 individuals worked in the coal pits and quarries, and there were also 38 engaged in retail or a skilled trade.[43] The number of agricultural workers had begun to fall by 1871, from 162 to 147, but coal production now employed 60, and 29 parishioners worked for the railway. The proportion of retail and skilled tradespeople had almost doubled, and most lived around the village centre, denoted 'Church End'. 'Hall End', the less densely populated northern half of the parish, was still primarily agricultural.[44]

Building projects, such as church renovation and the re-development of Stanshawes Court, reflected the wealth of Yate's Victorian landowners, but concerns for the growing working population also stimulated the development of social institutions. The colliery proprietors helped to establish a nonconformist school in 1850, and canvassed the neighbourhood to encourage families to attend. They also promoted moral and intellectual education more broadly by starting a library and supporting mutual improvement and temperance societies.[45] A similar impetus underlay the National School, established in 1853 to provide education for children of the labouring poor.[46]

Further dramatic demographic changes followed the development of the aerodrome site during the 1914–18 war. Parnall Aircraft took over the former Royal Flying Corps (from 1918, Royal Air Force) depot in 1925, and in 1932 Newman Electrical Motors began production on the eastern side of the site.[47] Both factories impacted significantly on Yate's community, and prefigured the concerted urban development under way before 1960.

By c.1965–70, between 1,500 and 2,000 people were employed on each site.[48] Newman's, where, reputedly, 'you could always get a job', paid better wages than those for agricultural work.[49] The factories provided an important source of employment for the region generally. By the 1950s workers were bussed in from Bristol and across

38   See pp. 45–6.
39   GA, Q/RIa/164; Q/RI/164.
40   See pp. 8–10.
41   *Census,* 1831–81.
42   *Census,* 1831.
43   *Census,* 1841.
44   *Census,* 1841 and 1871.
45   See p. 85.
46   See pp. 80–3.
47   See pp. 55–6.
48   Ibid.
49   YHC, O/2 and 57 (Oral History Project).

south Gloucestershire,[50] and Newman's helped to relocate new workers in the parish.[51] A diverse workforce was created, with women employed on both sites in factory and clerical work, and postgraduate programmes and apprenticeships in engineering offered at Newman's.[52] The Yate factories were also among the first locally to employ Asian and Caribbean Commonwealth workers during the 1950s, as well as European wartime immigrants, and Hungarian refugees after 1956.[53] A strong occupational community grew up around the factories, encouraged by dances, sports days and other activities held at the company social clubs.[54]

This influx accelerated Yate's population growth, from 1,332 in 1921 to 2,321 in 1951, and stimulated the first phase of residential development after 1950.[55] Plans for urban expansion were formalised in 1959 to meet local housing demand and provide 'overspill' accommodation for Bristol. Yate was selected because of its transport links, economic productivity, and the 'well founded local tradition, which will help social life'.[56]

As the new town was built, the population rose from 3,898 in 1961 to 13,599 in 1981.[57] Local amenities expanded as the town grew, but their delivery was delayed; and the phased nature of building, governed by the path of celestine extraction and changes in planning ethos, resulted in what were seen as 'separate villages in one town'.[58] Yate was perceived to be losing its rural character, and becoming a poor area of cheap housing.[59] Many felt that the new estates eroded the occupational community engendered by the factories, and prevented the establishment of a homogeneous town identity. Incomers, however, preferred Yate as an alternative to city life. The new estates provided cheaper, more modern homes and local amenities, but still close to the countryside.[60]

The community association, established in 1962, and the new town council formed in the 1970s, worked hard to improve amenities and generate a civic identity.[61] The local boundary review in 1978 confirmed the tensions experienced by Yate's residents: 'The impact of the massive increase in population on the local communities without public facilities keeping pace with the private, commercial, and industrial development has given rise to pressures which, it is believed, are far greater even than those sustained by statutory new towns.' Re-drawing the boundaries was considered vital in consolidating the new town: 'Yate has become a community. To not recognise that now and to refuse to give it the exceptional status it requires is to perpetuate the current problem.'[62] In 1988 the parish boundary was changed to reflect Yate's 'purely urban character', clearly

50   YHC, Newman's folders, *Gazette* cutting *c.*1960; O/165.
51   YHC, O/165.
52   YHC, Newman's Folder, Engineering training brochure *c.*1965; see p. 56.
53   YHC, O/165 and 2.
54   YHC, O/2, 9, and 165; see p. 86.
55   TNA, ED 161/5728.
56   YHC, D/299/New Town brochure, 1959.
57   *Census,* 1961–81.
58   YHC, O/38.
59   YHC, O/34 and 38.
60   YHC, O/37.
61   http://www.charitycommission.gov.uk (accessed 27 Jan. 2015) 301659; YHC, D/302/1–4; see pp. 65–6.
62   GA, P 357a/PC/11/1/2, Local Government Boundary Commission Report, 443, 1983, app. B, submission 108.

demarcating the extent of the new town.[63] By 2001, Yate had 21,789 residents, although this total had fallen slightly to 21,603 in 2011.[64]

Charities and Poor Relief

A bequest of 4d. made in 1576 referred to a 'church howse' used to accommodate the parish poor.[65] This may have been the building appropriated as a parish poorhouse and still in use in 1777, when it accommodated 40 paupers.[66]

No endowed charities for the poor of Yate were established until 1722, when Edward Yate, a Malmesbury (Wilts.) clothier, entrusted £80 in his will to the rectors of Yate and Wickwar, and three other trustees; the income from this sum, invested in land, was intended for apprenticing poor boys from the parishes of Wickwar and Yate 'in London and not elsewhere.'[67] In 1815, £131 was invested in stock, returning an annual dividend of £3 18s. 6d.[68] An apprenticeship was procured when enough interest accrued, estimated to be c.£80 in 1826;[69] however, Yate was only entitled to an apprentice 'one turn in three with the parish of Wickwar.' A Yate boy was sent to London under the scheme c.1825.[70] The charity still functioned in 1864–5,[71] and from 1909 to c.1979 formed part of Wickwar Combined Charities, which had been lost by 2011.[72]

By her will of 1731, Martha White left £200 to be distributed to the poor of Sodbury and Yate.[73] By 1762, £250 had been expended on the poor of Chipping Sodbury and Yate parishes from a total profit and investment of £253 19s. 6d.[74] The charity was recorded in 1828, but 'nothing [had] been received under it for a great many years.'[75]

In 1733 Daniel Belsire granted an annuity of £2 10s. issuing from Hall End farm to Yate churchwardens and overseers. The farm's proprietors or tenants were to distribute it in doles to Yate poor, 'as should most want the same, having or not having alms of the said parish'.[76] In 1786 and 1864–5, £2 10s. was distributed to the poor annually,[77] although the Charity Commissioners doubted in 1828 that it was of any beneficial purpose, as little care was paid to the nature of the claimants' cases, and the sums distributed were so

---

63   GA, P 357a/PC/11/1/2, app. B, submission 101, 53.
64   *Census,* 2001, 2011.
65   GDR wills, 1576/36.
66   *Poor Law Abs.*(1777), 355.
67   *17th Rep. Com. Char.* (1826–7) 386; BRO, P St MY/Ch/4.
68   *Rep. Charitable Donations* II (Parl. Papers 1820 (29)), p. 19.
69   *17th Rep. Com. Char.* (1826–7), 386.
70   *18th Rep. Com. Char.* (1828), 320.
71   *Endowed Charities Digest* (1867–8), 72.
72   GA, D 4952; http://www.charitycommission.gov.uk (accessed 20 Oct. 2014).
73   *Abstract of Returns of Charitable Donations* (Parl. Papers 1816 (511), pp. 414–15; *17th Rep. Com. Char.* (1826–7), 385.
74   *Returns of Char. Donations* (1816) 414–15.
75   *18th Rep. Com. Char.* (1828) 320.
76   Ibid.
77   *Returns of Char. Donations* (1816) 414–15; *Endowed Charities Digest* (1867–8), 72.

Figure 16 *The Chipping Sodbury Union workhouse, situated in Yate, designed by leading workhouse architects Scott and Moffatt.*

'trifling' owing to the large number of parishioners attending.[78] In 1970 Belsire's charity formed part of Yate United Charities, which continued in 2014.[79]

In 1739, Thomas Stokes, of Stanshawes manor, made two bequests of £100 each, for the poor and for apprenticing children.[80] The latter was believed lost in 1786, and family members could not give details regarding the trust for the former, as Stokes had died on his return from the West Indies.[81] In 1828 it was considered lost.[82]

Mason's charity was the largest established in the parish. Adding to a bequest by his wife Esther, William Mason, former rector of Yate, left £30 to the poor in 1741.[83] His son Benjamin gave £350 in his will of 1758 to augment the trust. The rector and churchwardens administered the charity, which stipulated that additional trustees must live within ten miles of Yate and adhere to the protestant religion.[84] In 1761 a house and 16 a. of land were bought for £330 to produce an income for ten poor housekeepers of the parish, 'resident and not otherwise in receipt of alms', every December.[85] It returned an income of £18 in 1786.[86] In 1815 the charity lands were exchanged for Warren's tenement, held by the lords of Yate manor; the farm included a house with garden, a barn, and approximately 17 a. of land. In 1828 the holding was let to one tenant at £32

78 *Endowed Charities Digest* (1867–8), 72.
79 http://www.charitycommission.gov.uk (accessed 27 Jan. 2015) 203164.
80 *Returns of Char. Donations* 1816, pp. 414–15.
81 Ibid.
82 *18th Rep. Com. Char.* (1828), 320.
83 TNA, PROB 11/730/99.
84 *18th Rep. Com. Char.* (1828), 321.
85 Ibid.
86 *Returns of Char. Donations* (1816), 414–15.

annually.[87] An additional investment of £265 12s., yielding £7 10s., was recorded in 1864, when the farm was let for £48 5s; the total income was then £56 4s. 4d.[88] The charity retained Warren's farm in 1877, along with a wharf near Yate Station and £459 in three per cent consols.[89]

In 1942 disbursements were made at Whitsuntide, and supported local hospitals, children entering service or skilled labour, and to pay school fees, as well as continuing to aid 'poor housekeepers' not in receipt of parochial relief.[90] Of the total income of £84, £30 was granted to five hospitals, including the cottage hospital in Yate, and to the Nursing Association. It was agreed to reduce provision to housekeepers, since by 1942 up to 40 were claiming.[91] From 1970 the Mason charity formed part of Yate United Charities.[92]

In 1760 John Walker bequeathed the profits of a plot of land, estimated at £1 annually, for 'Bibles and Testaments to the poor';[93] but in 1786 the bequest was considered 'unpaid'.[94] In 1828 the Charity Commissioners suggested advantage had been taken of the statute of mortmain, obviating the will's provisions.[95]

John Atwell bequeathed £90 in 1762 to apprentice poor boys of Yate within the parish.[96] With only £63 being paid, £27 from Mason's legacy was used to support the purchase of land. In 1828 the parish possessed this land and the churchwardens let it to a yearly tenant for £7 10s.[97] Atwell's charity continued to support education and training in Yate, and from 1944 formed a constituent of the Davis, Atwell or Wills charity, which remained active in 2014.[98] No record of Davis's charity was recorded before 1864, when it returned £5 12s. 9d. on an investment of £187 19s. 6d. for apprenticing boys in Yate.[99] In 2013 the combined charity offered grants to young people under 21, living in Yate, starting college, university or entering training.[100]

Atwell's charity may have supported the parish vestry in putting out boys and girls to work locally between 1815 and 1820 or later. The vestry stipulated terms of work, wages and clothing,[101] and agreed, annually or biannually, monthly allowances made to poor individuals and families. From 1803, only outdoor relief was made in Yate, suggesting that the poorhouse was no longer used.[102] Annual expenditure on the poor decreased from c.£407 in 1813 to £246 in 1815, but the number of regular claimants was relatively static at around 35, in addition to 15–20 occasional claimants.[103] Most requests were

87   *18th Rep. Com. Char.* (1828), 321.
88   *Endowed Charities Digest* (1867–8), 72.
89   BRO P.St MY/Ch/3c.
90   Ibid.
91   Ibid.
92   http://www.charitycommission.gov.uk (accessed 27 Jan. 2015), 203164.
93   *Returns of Char. Donations* (1816), 414–15; *18th Rep. Com. Char.* (1828), 321.
94   *Returns of Char. Donations* (1816), 414–15.
95   *18th Rep. Com. Char.* (1828), 321.
96   *Returns of Char. Donations* (1816), 414–15; *18th Rep. Com. Char.* (1828) 321–2.
97   *18th Rep. Com. Char.* (1828) 322.
98   http://www.charitycommission.gov.uk (accessed 27 Jan. 2015), 311482.
99   *Endowed Charities Digest* (1867–8), 72.
100   http://www.yatetowncouncil.gov.uk/yate-community/community-charities/ (accessed 21 Jan. 2015).
101   BRO P.St MY/V/1/a.
102   *Poor Law Abstract* (1803, 1818).
103   *Poor Law Abstract* (1818).

for clothes, rent and wages, but the largest allowance between 1815 and 1830 was £10 to William Thomas in 1818, to allow him to build a house and relocate his family to Wales. The parish was thereby relieved from paying Thomas £1 4s. monthly, the largest allowance that year.[104]

Table 5 *Annual expenditure on the poor, Yate 1776–1829*[105]

	Annual Expenditure		Annual Expenditure
1776	£211	1825	£361
1783–5	£173	1826	£415
1803	£282	1827	£341
1813	£407	1828	£323
1815	£246	1829	£296

The annual cost of poor relief in Yate increased from 1815, peaking in 1826 at £415 3s.,[106] indicating the parish was not immune to the pressures of agricultural depression following the Napoleonic Wars. Regular payments made by the vestry reflect this increase, from *c.*36 monthly in 1819 to *c.*48 in the first half of 1825; although the largest single payments fell from £1 to 12s.[107] Total annual expenditure decreased from 1827, to £296 in 1829,[108] but the number of regular claimants began to grow again during 1830.[109]

In 1836 Yate parish entered the new Chipping Sodbury Poor Law Union, which extended over Grumbalds Ash hundred and most of Pucklechurch hundred, including Frampton Cotterell, Doynton, Iron Acton and Marshfield.[110] In the same year, 26 Yate inhabitants were granted weekly relief of between 1s. and 4s. 6d., of whom 11 were over 65 and five were children.[111]

Initially the union used three poorhouses. Hawkesbury's poorhouse could accommodate 70 adults and served the upper division; the parishes of the union's lower division, including Yate, used the workhouse on Wickwar common and the poorhouse at Iron Acton, with accommodation for 40 and 60 adults respectively.[112] Concerns over their inadequacy were expressed from the outset; provision for a new workhouse was outlined in the original application to the Poor Law commissioners, but a motion to the guardians to build a new institution in April 1836 failed.[113] In July further anxiety was expressed at the 'internal arrangement and regulation' of the workhouses, with particular regard to 'the moral and religious instruction' of the inmates.[114] Another motion for new provision failed in June 1837, but by February 1838 'the want of work from the continuance of the

104 BRO P.St MY/V/1/a.
105 *Poor Law Abstract* (1803, 1818, 1830).
106 *Poor Law Abstract* (1830).
107 BRO P.St MY/V/1/a.
108 *Poor Law Abstract* (1830).
109 BRO P.St MY/V/1/a.
110 TNA, MH 12/3962.
111 GA, G/SO/8a/1.
112 Ibid.
113 TNA, MH 12/3962; GA, G/SO/8a/1.
114 GA, G/SO/8a/1.

severe weather' prompted the union to request the commissioners to suspend the rules prohibiting outdoor relief to able-bodied men, having only 'very imperfect workhouse accommodation and no employment for such description of paupers'.[115] The elderly at Hawkesbury poorhouse had already been transferred to Iron Acton in January due to overcrowding. In February Robert Neale, Assistant Commissioner, succeeded in passing a motion to build a union workhouse for 250 paupers.[116]

The site of the new building, designed by leading workhouse architects of the period, George Gilbert Scott and William Bonython Moffatt,[117] was east of Yate village centre on the south side of the main road to Chipping Sodbury.[118] A departure from typical workhouse architecture, it rejected the simplicity and economy of Georgian design for a Tudor-inspired style.[119] Scott and Moffatt advocated this to avoid giving a 'prisonlike appearance' to an establishment intended to be 'less a place of restraint than an asylum rendered necessary by misfortune'.[120] Formed of two (subsequently three) detached buildings, its entrance was a gabled archway in the north range facing the road, flanked by guardians' boardroom to the east and schoolroom to the west. The main range comprised a three-storey master's residence, flanked by two-storey accommodation for male paupers to the east, and women's quarters to the west.[121] From the elevated position of his rooms the master could survey both the entrance yard and the yard to the rear of the accommodation.[122] The later third range may date from 1847, and (following other designs by Scott and Moffatt) was probably an infirmary.[123]

In 1841 the workhouse housed 127 paupers, 125 in 1871, and 71 in 1881,[124] of whom 16 belonged to Yate parish.[125] Although out-relief was avoided where possible, the union still supported individuals outside the workhouse. In 1852 James Hobbs of Yate was granted up to £15 to enable him to emigrate to Australia with his wife and five children.[126]

In 1853 the old poorhouse was sold to enable the construction of a new church school.[127] After 1930 the union workhouse became a public assistance institution. Renamed Ridgewood c.1948 it was used as a county council residential home until the 1970s.[128] It was then turned into Avon County Council Social Services offices in 1982,[129] and in 2014 part of the site was the Ridgewood Community Centre.[130]

---

115 TNA, MH 12/3962.
116 GA, G/SO/8a/2.
117 K. Morrison, 'The New Poor Law Workhouses of George Gilbert Scott and William Bonython Moffatt', *Architectural History*, 40 (1997), 184–203.
118 OS Map 6", Glos. LXIX.SW (1886 edn).
119 Morrison, 'New Poor Law Workhouses', 190; Verey and Brooks, *Glos.* II, 827; site visit, 2012.
120 Morrison, 'New Poor Law Workhouses', 190.
121 Verey and Brooks, *Glos.* II, 827; OS Map 6", Glos. LXIX.SW (1886 edn).
122 Morrison, 'New Poor Law Workhouses', 191–2.
123 Verey and Brooks, *Glos.* II, 827; P. Alcock, *Whispers from the Workhouse* (1992); Morrison, 'New Poor Law Workhouses', 190–1.
124 *Census,* 1841, 1871, 1881.
125 *Census,* 1881.
126 GA, G/SO/8a/4.
127 Ibid.; see pp. 77–8.
128 GA, K 910/1/3; OS Map 25", ST 7281 (1955, 1970 edns); P. Alcock, *Whispers from the Workhouse* (1992).
129 NHL, no. 1128772, Ridgewood, Yate offices of Avon County Council Social Services: 12 Feb. 2015.
130 Local Authority Publishing, *Yate Town Guide* (2013), 26; local inf.

Education

In 1819 no endowment for education, nor any educational institution, was recorded in the parish.[131] A building of c.1839 in late medieval style immediately south-east of the churchyard was referred to as the 'school house' in 1852,[132] although no earlier evidence has been found for a school in Yate village.[133] A schoolmistress was provided, however, for the workhouse children from 1839 and a Sunday school was held in the parish church before 1851.[134] Rival day schools were established in the parish: a British (nonconformist) school on North Road, immediately east of Yate colliery, in 1850; and a National (Anglican) school just south of the parish church between 1852 and 1855.[135] A private preparatory school, managed by Miss Ann Neale, opened in the village before 1856.[136]

Yate British School

The impetus for founding the British School stemmed largely from local coal interests. Handel Cossham, manager of Yate colliery, proposed the scheme, and was joined on the founding committee by Christopher Keeling and Robert Staley, and latterly Samuel Long, all proprietors of mining operations in Yate.[137] Cossham laid the school's foundation stone in September 1850, and in November Jacob Pegler of Ebley was appointed master on an initial annual salary of £55. A teacher's residence was provided adjacent to the school.[138] Before it opened tracts were distributed among the colliery community, emphasising 'the importance of education and stating the terms and rules of the school'; a public meeting and tea were held, reportedly attended by 2,000 supporters. The school opened to 60 boys and girls in June 1851.[139]

The building contained a schoolroom, and an infants' room, and had a playground.[140] It was also used for community meetings from 1851 until 1860 or later, and a Sunday school in 1861. In 1855 it hosted a community 'circulating library',[141] and annual trips to the Malvern Hills or Weston-super-Mare were arranged for the scholars. The committee negotiated discounted fares with the Midland Railway, which operated the line through Yate, and in 1865 children from Pucklechurch Sunday school were allowed to join the trip.[142]

From its inception until 1879 the school relied on voluntary funding from collections made at chapel meetings in the surrounding parishes, regular donations from individuals, and the fees or 'school pence' paid by the pupils' families. Despite being classed a British School there is no record of funding from the British and Foreign

---

131 *Educ. of Poor Digest* (1819), 318 and 326.
132 GA, D 2186/140; TNA, ED 49/10639, Verey and Brooks, *Glos.* II, 826.
133 See p. 80.
134 *Religious Census,* 1851.
135 See pp. 80–3.
136 *Post Office Dir. Glos.* (1856 edn), 394.
137 GA, S M381/M1.
138 GA, S M381/M1.
139 Ibid.
140 GA, C/AE/R/4/392.
141 GA, S M381/M1.
142 Ibid.

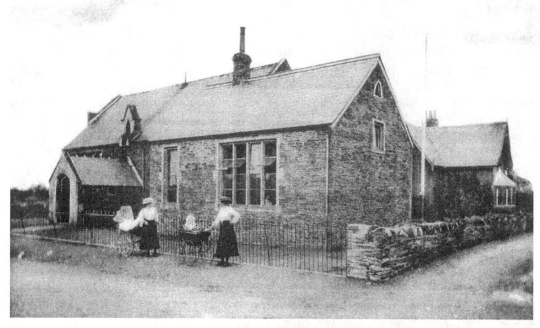

Figure 17 *Yate's British School, opened in 1850 (photographed c.1910).*

School Society.[143] In 1855 the managers expressed concern at 'the low state of the school', and impressed the teacher to visit all parents over the following month. The average weekly attendance increased from 73 in 1855 to a monthly average regularly over 100 in 1856. In 1858 it was reported that attendance, and the progress of the school, was 'going on favourable'. But in 1859 Handel Cossham resigned from the governing committee, 'declining longer to support the school in any way', and the following year attendance contracted again, and the school recorded an income deficit of £10 12s. In 1861 the management committee agreed to retrench annual expenditure and Aaron Turner, the master, volunteered to forego a salary increase. Despite his detachment, Cossham offered to sell the teacher's house to the committee in 1862 for £100, to be invested in a trust to support the school. A lack of capital delayed the matter until January 1866 when the sale was finally completed.[144]

In 1871 the management committee considered, but ultimately deferred, placing the school under government control. When the long-serving master, Aaron Turner, resigned in 1879, they agreed that it should become a public elementary school, liable to inspections but also eligible for government grants. Part of the grant was included in the terms used to secure the new master, a Mr Parkinson.[145]

In 1870 the school could accommodate 175 children. Because it stood on the edge of the parish, more than a mile from the village centre, it was 'largely attended by children from other parishes'; it was estimated that only 35 pupils were from Yate.[146] When it

143 GA, S M381/M1; TNA, ED 21/29051.
144 GA, S M381/M1.
145 GA, S M381/M1; YHC, British School log book (1879–1927).
146 TNA, ED 2/190.

opened as a public elementary school in 1879, it had 130 children on roll, with a monitor and monitress to assist the master.[147]

Arriving in September 1879, Parkinson was unimpressed by the pupils' learning, complaining that 'grammar and geography have been almost if not entirely neglected'.[148] By November he still could not address these deficiencies, as the schoolchildren's arithmetic required so much attention.[149] Despite these concerns the first government report in March 1880 was glowing; the inspector was unprepared 'for the perfect order, the regular organisation and drill, still less the very creditable results of examination'. The school was viewed as an exception to the poor conditions normally found in institutions recently placed under government control; and credit was given to both Parkinson and his predecessor, Turner.[150]

Average weekly attendance rose during 1881 from 114 to 142, when small cash prizes were given to the most regular attenders, and numbers stabilized at c.137 in 1882.[151] Bad weather regularly affected attendance; storms prevented all the boys travelling from Westerleigh in April 1880, and a measles outbreak closed the school for a fortnight. In 1886 diphtheria claimed at least two schoolchildren and caused several families to keep their children at home. Annual events such as Chipping Sodbury fair and Iron Acton club walk reduced attendance, and through summer and early autumn fruit picking, haymaking and harvest diverted children from their studies.[152] In February 1888, after Yate colliery closed causing great distress, attendance by children from affected families dropped, and the school struggled to collect their fees. Several parents left Yate to seek work in south Wales.[153]

By 1900 there were 223 children on roll and the average attendance was 169. The curriculum had expanded to include physics and elementary science, and singing, drawing, needlework and physical exercises were also taught.[154] Between c.1905 and 1925, however, the school began to contract.[155]

Table 6 *British School attendance, 1900–25*

	Registered	Attendance
1900	223	169
1905	180	163
1910	157	143
1915	156	137
1920	142	128
1925	136	115

147 YHC, British School log book (Oct. 1879).
148 Ibid. (Sept. 1879).
149 Ibid. (Nov. 1879).
150 Ibid.; HMI report, 1880.
151 YHC, British School log book (1881–2).
152 Ibid. (1879–1902).
153 Ibid., 1888, f. 117.
154 YHC, British School log Book, curriculum scheme (1900).
155 TNA, ED 161/5257.

Reports on teaching standards were generally positive, but concerns that the building was unsuitable were raised in 1901–2, and again in 1926.[156] Additional accommodation for the older, mixed children was constructed in 1903,[157] but in 1929 the managers were warned that government support would be withdrawn if necessary alterations and improvements were not made, and subsequently an inspector reported the school as 'dingy, dirty and dilapidated'. In consequence the managers and trustees agreed to transfer the school to local authority control in 1930.[158]

Renamed Yate Council School in July 1931, with a £2,000 grant for expansion, by 1932 the large schoolroom was divided into classrooms and new facilities provided for staff and schoolchildren. Adjoining land was bought for use as a garden in 1933, and in 1934–5 a handicraft room to be shared with five other local schools was added.[159] This facility enabled practical instruction, which supported the growth of engineering manufacture in the area, and was considered invaluable 'to those boys who pass into industries where precision and an understanding of working drawings are of prime importance'.[160] During the 1930s attendance remained stable at c.114, with c.124 registered,[161] and between 1942 and 1945 ten evacuees (predominantly from London) were accommodated.[162] From 1953 the school taught children only up to the age of 11.[163]

Yate National School

Yate's rector, churchwardens and leading inhabitants applied in 1852 to build a school for 40 boys and 40 girls.[164] The children of the labouring poor, claimed Revd George Ludford Harvey, risked falling 'into habits of profligacy, there being no school connected with the Church!' Harvey himself contributed £100 towards an estimated total of £406 for the school and master's residence, which was matched by a local subscription, and a further £30 was granted from Samuel Wilson Warneford's charity.[165] The Committee of Council on Education and the National Society helped to cover the shortfall, giving £105 and £28 respectively. Harvey expected annual funding to be met by a subscription of £45, and £5 from the school pence.[166]

The school was erected in 1855 on the western perimeter of the churchyard, opposite the old so-called 'school house'.[167] It occupied the site of the former poorhouse,[168] and was built in Tudor style, in keeping with the church, with north and south porches, the south crowned by a bellcote.[169] Separate classrooms were provided for boys and girls, and the playground to the rear was also segregated.[170]

---

156 YHC, British School log book (1900–10); TNA, ED 21/29051.
157 GA, C/AE/R/4/392 county surveyor's report 1903.
158 TNA, ED 21/29051.
159 Ibid.; TNA, ED 70/902.
160 Ibid. ED 21/51987.
161 TNA, ED 161/5727.
162 GA, C/AE/V/1/4.
163 TNA, ED 161/5727.
164 TNA, ED 103/26/34, ff. 755–65.
165 Ibid.; *ODNB*, s.a. Warneford, Samuel Wilson (1763–1855), philanthropist (accessed 19 Feb. 2015).
166 TNA, ED 103/26/34, ff. 755–65.
167 GA, D 2186/140; Verey and Brooks, *Glos.* II, 826; site visit, 2012.
168 See pp. 72, 74.
169 GA, D 2186/140; Verey and Brooks, *Glos.* II, 826; site visit, 2012.
170 GA, D 2186/140.

Figure 18 *Original architect's elevation of Yate National School, 1853.*

In 1864 average attendance was 68 but, as with the British School, numbers fluctuated with bad weather, illness and harvest work,[171] not to mention local festivals and attractions. In May 1866 the circus at Sodbury admitted schoolchildren for a penny; with only 20 schoolchildren the master capitulated and declared a half-holiday.[172] In 1867 there were 100 pupils on roll, and another 39 attended evening school.[173]

In 1870 the school accommodated between 70 and 100 pupils, but then the room was 'overflowing'. Citing population growth and the few parish children attending the British School, an additional classroom was recommended.[174] Despite the managers supporting expansion, by 1875 the plans were dismissed because, according to the rector, the ratepayers were unwilling to fund it. He conceded that it was unnecessary, since children from the more dispersed north of the parish attended schools in Rangeworthy and Wickwar, and elsewhere in Yate numbers were divided equally between the British and National Schools.[175]

Table 7 *National School attendance, 1890–1911*[176]

	Annual Average
1890	60
1895	70
1900	83
1905	105
1910	134
1911	140

171 YHC, National School log book (1863–1887).
172 Ibid., 22 May 1866.
173 Ibid., Oct. 1867.
174 TNA, ED 2/190.
175 Ibid.
176 YHC, National School log book (1887–1912).

Average attendance increased steadily after *c.*1890 until 1898,[177] when a small decrease in 1899 prompted the rector to express regret that Yate parish children were attending other schools. Numbers recovered in 1900, and the National School began admitting children from Westerleigh (formerly attending the British School) and the relatively distant hamlet of Yate Rocks, as well as some children from the union workhouse.[178]

As school population mirrored village expansion between 1902 and 1939, so its facilities required periodic re-organisation. The infant accommodation was enlarged in 1902,[179] and in 1910 the classrooms were re-ordered and improved lighting, heating and sanitation installed.[180] Despite recognising that the neighbourhood was likely to continue growing, particularly after *c.*1910 when new chemical works opened, the school was only considered fit to accommodate 139 schoolchildren, rather than 165 as previously assessed. The school board expected the managers to transfer it to local authority control, since they could not afford improvements; but a contribution from Chipping Sodbury guardians allowed the work to be completed in 1911. The school could then admit 176 children, and had 153 registered in 1912.[181]

Although total pupil numbers decreased to *c.*100 after 1918, 'marked fluctuations' in the school population as the village expanded caused problems. In 1926 it was noted that 'nearly half the present scholars [had] been admitted during the last three years', and in 1929–30 a further 81 children were registered. The inspector confirmed the strain on teaching staff contending with 'a large number of migratory children . . . as well as an influx of younger children from new council houses in the neighbourhood.'[182] A fifth classroom was added in 1938.[183] Despite its rapid growth, academic achievement was maintained.[184] In addition to the three Rs, history, geography, music and art were taught; the children also cultivated a garden.[185] From 1936 they were taught handicrafts at the British School's new facility.[186]

Evacuees to the parish between 1940 and 1945 placed further pressure on its schools. The National School took 21 children, largely from London and the Home Counties. In 1944 the residents of St Andrew's Children's Home in New Malden (Surrey) were housed at The Lawns, opposite the National School, after a bombing raid destroyed their premises. The National School master highlighted the impossibility of accommodating any number of the 27 evacuated children once they attained primary school age, having 197 children at the school already. One child from the home was admitted in 1945, however, having been adopted by a local family.[187]

In 1952 the National School was classified as voluntary-aided and renamed the Church of England school, and in 1953 it was restricted to primary education.[188]

177 YHC, National School log book (1887–1912).
178 Ibid. (1900).
179 GA, C/AE/R/4/391 county surveyor's report (1903); TNA, ED 21/6096.
180 TNA, ED 21/6096.
181 Ibid.
182 TNA, ED 21/29050.
183 TNA, ED 21/51986.
184 TNA, ED 21/29050.
185 TNA, ED 21/51986.
186 TNA, ED 161/5968.
187 GA, C/AE/V/1/4.
188 TNA, ED 161/5968.

It successfully resisted attempts in 1955 to reduce it to infant school status, and opposed plans to build a new primary school to serve the growing estates.[189] In 1965 Gloucestershire County Council was recommended to borrow £23,000 to purchase a new site, and from 1969 Yate Church of England school occupied a new larger building immediately east of the church, which was still used in 2014.[190]

Education and the New Town Development 1955–2014

The Ridge primary school, opened by Gloucestershire County Council in 1954, and offering 280 places to boys and girls, was the first new primary school built to meet the demands of urban expansion from *c.*1950. The council was responding to the increasing number of families attracted to the east of the parish by factories such as Parnall's, and to the anticipated Bristol overspill. Despite government concerns that building might outstrip population growth, the council asserted that the population movement was 'of such magnitude that there must be a very serious pressure in this area.'[191]

The new town plan in *c.*1959 formalised education provision by proposing that each of the five new estates would have a primary school.[192] Although notice had been given to build a school on the Aerodrome estate in 1955,[193] the plans were deferred in the face of local opposition, and to assess how far existing schools kept pace with demand; the school was not built.[194] Stanshawes Court junior school opened in 1965 on the new estate in south Yate,[195] and between *c.*1967 and *c.*1977, three more primary schools and a Roman Catholic school were established to serve the expanding area.[196] In north Yate infant and junior schools were also built in the Cranleigh Court area.[197]

Secondary schools were another consequence of the new town development. Plans for a secondary school in 1937–8, supported by the Church Senior Schools fund established by Arthur Headlam, Bishop of Gloucester, were never realised.[198] From 1953, Yate pupils over 11 years attended secondary schools elsewhere, including Chipping Sodbury secondary modern.[199] The Board of Education's Bristol overspill scheme envisaged three secondary schools for the Yate/Sodbury area, including a secondary modern and a technical school,[200] and provision for a school for children with special educational needs was included in the 1967 revised town plans.[201] As development progressed, King Edmund secondary modern school was opened at Sunridge Park in south Yate in 1966,[202]

189 Below; TNA, ED 161/5728; ED 161/5968.
190 TNA, ED 161/5968; YHC, D/2220; site visit, 2013.
191 TNA, ED 161/5728.
192 YHC, YHC, D/299/New Town Brochure (1959); see pp. 20–1.
193 TNA, ED 161/5733.
194 Ibid.
195 TNA, ED 161/5733.
196 GA, S 417; S 381/1; OS Map 1970 1:10,000, ST78SW.
197 OS Map 1970 1:10,000, ST78SW; *Gazette*, 14 Nov. 2012.
198 GDR, A 17/10/31–4.
199 TNA, ED 161/5968; ED 161/5727.
200 TNA, ED 161/5733.
201 YHC, D/296.
202 GA, K 484/281.

and Brimsham Green comprehensive in north Yate in 1977.[203] The Glevum special school was reformed as the Culverhill school in 1999.[204]

When South Gloucestershire unitary authority was created in 1996 education in Yate was reorganized. Under a policy supporting 'all-through' primary education, several infants and junior schools amalgamated and re-opened as primary schools between 2001 and 2009.[205] King Edmund school left local authority control in 2009 to become Yate International Academy, part of the Ridings Federation associated with the Ridings School, Winterbourne.[206] The academy also incorporated Woodlands primary 'phase' (replacing Stanshawes Court junior and Kingsgate infant schools), and so became the first academy in South Gloucestershire to provide education for three to 19 year olds.[207] In 2014 Yate had nine primary and two secondary schools.[208]

Social Life

A common alehouse existed in 1667/8, when Joan Belseire was prosecuted for keeping it without licence.[209] Yate had an inn with two guest beds and stabling for two horses in 1686,[210] perhaps a precursor of the White Lion, which was open in 1798 when the local friendly society met there.[211] The White Lion continued to be a hub for community activity throughout the 19th century,[212] and the Beaufort Hunt met and had stables there.[213] The late 16th-century building was altered in the 18th and 20th centuries, and continued trading in 2013.[214] Other public houses followed: the White Hart by 1852, and the Railway Hotel on Station Road by 1856; and the Swan inn by 1897, when three beer retailers were also listed.[215] In 1939 the Railway Hotel and Swan inn were trading, along with the Cross Keys (a former beerhouse) and a beer retailer.[216] In 2014 there were ten public houses in Yate.[217]

The friendly society registered in 1798 had a membership of 147 in 1813–15.[218] In 1861, when it had 160 members, its anniversary was celebrated at the White Lion,

203 OS Map 1989 1:10,000, ST78SW; Brimsham Green school information for applicants (2014).
204 http://www.education.gov.uk/edubase/establishment/summary.xhtml?urn=131808 (accessed 27 Jan. 2015).
205 South Glos. Council, *Consultation Paper Autumn 2007, Dept. for Children and Young People*; http://www.education.gov.uk/edubase/establishment/summary.xhtml?urn=132199; http://www.education.gov.uk/edubase/establishment/summary.xhtml?urn=135783 (both accessed 27 Jan. 2015).
206 *Bristol Post*, 3 and 9 Apr. 2009; http://www.trfyia.org.uk (accessed 12 Feb. 2015).
207 http://www.trfyia.org.uk/woodlands (accessed Apr. 2014).
208 http://www.southglos.gov.uk (accessed Apr. 2014).
209 GA, Q/SIb/1.
210 TNA, WO 30/49.
211 GA, Q/RSf/2.
212 *Slater's Dir. Glos.* (1852 edn), 154; *Kelly's Dir. Glos.* (1868, 1897 edns).
213 *Bristol Mercury*, 17 Oct. 1857, 9 Nov 1878; YHC, Murray Dowding Collection, Yate Hounds in front of the White Lion *c.*1910.
214 NHL, no. 1321156, The White Lion, 12 Feb. 2015; site visits, 2012 and 2013.
215 *Post Office Dir. Glos.* (1856 edn), 394; *Kelly's Dir. Glos.* (1897 edn), 367–8.
216 *Kelly's Dir. Glos.* (1939 edn), 389–90.
217 Local inf.
218 *Poor Law Abstract* (1818).

Figure 19 *A meeting of the hounds outside the White Lion public house, c.1910.*

attended by Revd W.C. Randolph, lord of Yate manor, and Revd George Ludford Harvey, rector.[219] The society still existed in 1880.[220]

The developing colliery community used the British School for various communal activities with a strong emphasis on self-improvement. From its inception the schoolroom was used for preaching on the Sabbath, and housed a circulating library from 1855. Subscribers paid 1*d*. per book or 1*s*. quarterly in advance; loans were for two weeks, with a daily fine of ½*d*. if overdue. Subscriptions were reduced for local women and children, and male library members were encouraged to join the mutual improvement society. In 1858 Handel Cossham secured the use of the schoolroom for temperance meetings.[221] A reading room, first proposed at the British School before 1851, was opened in the parish in 1896, paid for by a public subscription.[222]

In 1914 a new permanent building was erected for the Yate and District Young Men's Association on Station Road.[223] This hall was subsequently dedicated in memory of Francis Frederick Fox of Yate House.[224] In 1934 a parish hall was built next door, and was used as a cinema between 1942 and 1956 or later.[225]

Yate Women's Institute was founded in 1925 and continued to meet until 2003.[226] The parish church supported a Mothers' Union branch before 1929[227] and had established a young wives' group by 1965;[228] these organisations proved especially useful to women

219 *Bristol Mercury*, 1 June 1861.
220 *Bristol Mercury*, 31 May 1880.
221 GA, S M381/M1.
222 *Kelly's Dir. Glos.* (1897 edn), 367–8.
223 YHC, D/2025/2.
224 *Kelly's Dir. Glos.* (1914 edn), 386; see pp. 29–30.
225 *Kelly's Dir. Glos.* (1939 edn), 389; Verey and Brooks, *Glos.* II, 826; Glos. Colln. SR 649/33391GS, *c*.1956.
226 YTC, newsletter, July 2004.
227 YHC, MDC photograph, 1929.
228 YHC, photograph of Church Young Wives' group 1965.

Figure 20 *A Christmas party at Newman Industries, c.1950.*

moving into the developing new town.[229] In 2013 St Mary's continued to host Yate
Mothers' Union and other community groups.[230] Yate and District Townswomen's Guild
was formed in 1985 and registered as a charity in 2003. A morning and evening meeting
were established, but the latter had closed by 2008.[231]

Yate Rovers Football Club, established in 1906, was supported by the YMCA from
*c.*1933, and from 1946 was known as Yate YMCA. It was one of the founding teams of
the Gloucester County League in 1958, when it was renamed Yate Town FC; it remained
active in 2014.[232] In 1918 the Royal Flying Corps site was commandeered for a village
sports day.[233] Although an application to fund a permanent playing field at Yate was
rejected in 1939, Newman Industries had supported the development of a sports ground
with pavilion west of the factory by 1955.[234] The company also established a social club
near the site on Station Road, which held regular dances and parties for its staff.[235]

229 YHC, O/162, J&ME.
230 See p. 105.
231 GA, D12941; http://www.charitycommission.gov.uk (accessed 27 Jan. 2015), 1095894 and 1099005.
232 YHC, D/218/1; YHC/2026/3; local inf.
233 YHC, MDC RAF sports day, 1918.
234 GA, C/AC/C6/5/1; OS Maps 25", ST 7082 (1955 edn).
235 YHC, Newman's, photographs *c.*1950–65, YHC, O/2 and O/9.

The 1959 plan for the new town promised 'new shops, new schools, new parks and playing fields' to accompany residential development.[236] Playing fields on the northern edge of Westerleigh common, and Kingsgate Park, formerly the grounds of Stanshawes Court, were developed by 1970.[237] In 1978 the town council administered cricket and football pitches, and tennis courts adjacent to the Westerleigh common playing fields; there was also a municipal tennis court on the Ridge estate.[238] A popular campaign in 1988 defeated attempts to sell Westerleigh common, which would have risked losing it as a public space.[239] In 2003, a skate park was opened at Peg Hill (north Yate).[240]

Yate shopping centre, opened in 1965, offered important social amenities for the growing new town.[241] By including shopping facilities, town planners aimed to provide structured activities for women and young people, in particular, alleviating the anticipated boredom of the former and the potential for delinquency in the latter.[242] An entertainment centre, opened in the shopping complex by 1970, offered dances, games and film screenings; but it struggled to attract the younger and less affluent families moving to new estates in south Yate.[243] The 'Stars and Stripes Club', opened in the centre in 1976, proved more popular, and continued to trade as 'Spirals' and then 'Time' throughout the 1980s and 1990s.[244] A library, and the first phase of the Southwolds leisure centre, had been constructed next to the shopping centre by 1976.[245] By 1990 a health centre, social security services, and bases for the local emergency services were established in the shopping centre complex, which continued to be the focus for Yate's public and commercial facilities in 2014.[246]

When the 19th-century church school building closed in 1969 it was redeveloped as a youth centre for Yate's adolescent population.[247] A second centre, subsequently part of the St Nicholas family centre, was built in the same year in Abbotswood, south Yate.[248] Despite these facilities, concerns were expressed about a lack of activities for young people as the town continued to grow. In 1996, responding to complaints that the parish youth were 'running riot', the leisure centre hosted a new youth night, encouraging engagement with sport, music and the arts.[249] In 1997, 300 young people attended the youth centre at the St Nicholas family complex, which also provided outreach workers to offer friendship and support to children not attending organised groups.[250] The distinctive 'Armadillo' building, or Yate Youth Café, opened in 2011 through a partnership between

236 YHC, D/299/A.
237 YHC, D/296; OS 1970 1:10 000, ST78SW.
238 YHC, D/302/1–4.
239 GA, D 6822/70; see pp. 65–6.
240 YHC/e/601/177.
241 See Shopping Centre, pp. 22–3.
242 G. Ortolano, 'Planning the Urban Future in 1960s Britain', *Historical Journal*, 54 (2) (2011), 495–7.
243 YHC, *Glos. Life*, 1970
244 YTC, Yate Town Vision (2008); YHC, *Gazette*, 5 Sept. 1997; photographs of Stars and Stripes, 1976–7.
245 YHC, D/3/2.
246 YHC, D/2458 Yate and District Community Newspaper; http://www.yateshoppingcentre.co.uk (accessed 12 Feb. 2015).
247 See p. 83.
248 YHC, D/2220 school and youth project brochure.
249 *Bristol Observer*, 31 Oct. 1996.
250 Ibid., 6 Mar. 1997.

the town and unitary authority councils. In addition to the café, the venue served as a cinema.[251]

In 1995 the town council funded the foundation of the Yate & District Heritage Centre. The centre, relocated in 2000 to former stables near St Mary's church, provided information and local history to the community, as well as an exhibition space and venue for groups and events, including the local branch of the University of the Third Age and the annual Yate International Festival.[252]

251 *Gazette*, 24 July 2013; http://www.yatearmadillo.co.uk; site visit, 2012.
252 http://www.yateheritage.co.uk; site visits, 2012–14.

UNTIL 1541, WHEN IT BECAME a member of the newly constituted diocese of Gloucester, the parish of Yate lay within Worcester diocese. It was transferred to the diocese of Bristol in 1976.[1] A church had been established within the settlement by the 12th century.[2] Little remained of the Norman church after substantial rebuilding during the 15th, 16th and 19th centuries; these campaigns coincided with other developments in the parish, notably the renovation of Yate Court, and similarly impressive phases of construction in the late Victorian period.[3]

From at least 1603 the rectory was considered a valuable one;[4] and after its separation from the manor of Yate in the 17th century, it became a substantial manor in its own right.[5] The division of these two centres of local authority, coupled with periods when the manorial lords of Yate and the parish clergy were absent, may account for the growth of nonconformity within the parish from at least 1600. Certainly, before 1800, relations between the established church and Yate's freeholders, including some dissenters, were not always easy.[6]

Nonconformist congregations proliferated after 1800 as the settlement grew, and were frequently located around the industrial sectors of the parish or away from the village centre. The parish church retained its significance nevertheless, as is evident from the public support for the renovations made at the end of the 19th century. In response to the development of the new town and Yate's increasing population, the Anglican church was restructured and, reflecting the town's diverse community, a new Catholic church was founded.[7]

Early History and Status of the Parish Church

No archaeological or extant documentary evidence supports the suggestion that a minster was established at Yate when Westbury-on-Trym minster was founded in 716. References in charters now lost are ambiguous, and may refer only to the settlement at Westbury.[8] No church was recorded as part of the bishop of Worcester's estates at Yate in

---

1   *Fast. Eccl.* vol. 8; *London Gazette* Apr. 1976.
2   Verey and Brooks, *Glos.* II, 824.
3   See pp. 29–30.
4   *Eccl. Misc.* 65.
5   See pp. 91–3.
6   See pp. 99–100.
7   See pp. 105–6.
8   P. Couzens, *Annals of a Parish viz. Yate* (1990), 6; C. Heighway, *Anglo-Saxon Glos.* (1987) Appendix 1, 167; *VCH Glos.* II, 106; Finberg, *Early Charters of the West Midlands* (1961), 34, 38; see pp. 11–12.

1086.[9] However, the reincorporation of 12th-century materials, notably a small round-headed window in the west wall of the south transept of the parish church, suggests that the building is of Norman origin.[10] The first documentary reference to the church and rectory at Yate occurs in the register of Godfrey Giffard, Bishop of Worcester, in 1271.[11]

The medieval dedication of the church is not recorded. In c.1690 it was noted that the dedication was 'supposed to be to St John the Baptist';[12] but between 1735 and 1750 the church was ascribed to St Mary, and this was maintained into the 21st century.[13]

The ecclesiastical parish of Yate formed part of the deanery of Hawkesbury in the see of Worcester until 1541, when a new diocese based on Gloucester was established. Apart from a brief reversal between 1552 and 1554, Yate remained in the see of Gloucester until the diocese of Gloucester and Bristol was formed in 1836.[14] Bristol became an independent bishopric in 1897, but Yate did not fall within its jurisdiction until the parish was transferred from Gloucester in 1976.[15] It was then reconstituted as part of the benefice and parish of Yate New Town.[16] In 2014 the new town parish comprised St Mary's church, St Nicholas's church and family centre based at Abbotswood in south Yate, St Peter's church at Wapley and the church of St James the Great at Westerleigh. This parish formed part of Kingswood and South Gloucestershire deanery in the archdeaconry of Malmesbury, Bristol diocese.[17]

Patronage and Endowment

The Advowson

From the early 12th until the end of the 16th century, patronage of the parish church was dictated by the pattern of Yate's manorial lordship. The de Willingtons held the advowson with the manor from before 1311 until c.1352, when John de Willington's estates were under crown wardship during his minority.[18] The crown held the manor and advowson of Yate again c.1391–7, while John's heir (also John) was in the King's custody.[19] Although Isabel Beaumont, John's sister and heir, recovered the advowson along with the manor of Yate in 1397, the crown retained the right to the next presentation, which it made in 1402.[20] In 1501 the advowson passed with the manor to the Daubeneys, and then to the duke of Somerset, reverting once more to the crown on his attainder in 1552.[21]

9   *Domesday*, 452.
10   Site visit, 2013; Verey and Brooks, *Glos.* II, 824; F. Ashley, *History of Yate Church* (c.1997).
11   *Reg. Giffard* I, 47.
12   *Parsons's Notes*, 289.
13   *Benson's Surv.* 39; see below.
14   *Fasti. Eccl. Ang.* vols. 7 and 8; *Tax. Eccl.*; *Valor Eccl.*; GDR, A 2/3.
15   *London Gazette*, Apr. 1976; *Fast. Eccl.* vol. 8.
16   *Crockford's Clerical Dir.* (1977–9), 1321; ibid. (1980–2), 1332.
17   Diocese of Bristol, *Yate New Town Parish Profile* (2012–13), http://www.bristol.anglican.org/our-churches/kingswood-and-south-gloucestershire-deanery (accessed 28 Jan. 2015); see also p. 26.
18   *Reg.Reynolds* 88, 152; *Cal. Pat.* 1350–4, 25; see p. 26.
19   *Inq. p.m. Glos.* 1359–1413, 201–2; *Cal. Pat.* 1396–9, 263; see p. 26.
20   *Cal. Pat.* 1396–9, 263 (Nov. 1397); *Cal. Close* 1396–9 (Dec. 1397); *Cal. Pat.* 1401–5, 97 (May 1402).
21   *Glos. Feet of Fines 1360–1508*, 192–3; see p. 27.

In 1557 the manor and advowson were restored to James Bassett and his nephew Arthur, rightful heirs to the Beaumonts.[22] On Arthur's death in 1585, his son Robert was expected to inherit the manor and advowson, with the first presentation bequeathed to Robert's brother, Francis.[23] By virtue of the separation of advowson and manor, however, a caveat of 1572 asserted the right of Thomas Neale and Robert Baynham of Yate, as patrons of the church, to present.[24] This right was upheld in the same year when they presented Thomas Baynham to the rectory.[25] Between 1603 and 1638 the claim of the Baynhams as patrons of the church at Yate was assured when Robert Bassett granted the advowson to Adam Baynham, also of Yate.[26]

The Baynham (also Bainham) family of Yate, and latterly of Stogumber (Som.),[27] continued as patrons of Yate church until 1741, when Richard Wallington was instituted as rector on his own petition.[28] Wallington succeeded to the rectory manor and advowson on his marriage to Elizabeth Hodges, who had inherited the estate from her father, Robert Godwyn. The Godwyn and Baynham families were interrelated from 1661 or earlier.[29]

Between 1741 and 1896 the rectors of Yate held the advowson, which descended with the sale of the rectory manor. Thomas Tournay, rector between 1765 and 1795, purchased the fee simple and inheritance of the manor and advowson for £1,500 from Richard Wallington in 1760. In the same year Tournay granted patronage of the living to William Tournay for the next turn only, on the understanding that William would present Thomas to the living.[30] Thomas Tournay sold the manor and advowson to Richard John Hay of Cricklade (Wilts) in 1791 for £2,000. Hay was licensed as curate to the church at Yate by Tournay's nomination in 1793, and presented himself to the rectory in 1795.[31] In a similar manner William Stephen Goodenough purchased the living and estate from Hay in 1796, five years before Hay resigned. Goodenough was licensed as curate in 1799, and instituted as rector in 1801 by his mother, Ann Goodenough, from whom he inherited the advowson before 1838.[32] Goodenough sold the manor and advowson in 1839 to George Ludford Harvey, and he granted the next presentation to Lee Thornton, who presented Harvey to the rectory in 1843.[33] Edmund Pontifex purchased the manor and advowson from Harvey in 1869, who preferred his son Alfred to the rectory the same year. Alfred bought the fee simple of the advowson and rectory from the trustees of his father's will in 1870.[34] When Pontifex sold the manor and advowson to William Rhodes Emmott in 1896 clerical patronage at Yate came to an end.

22 *Cal. Pat.* 1563–6, II; GA, D 269B/T25, copy of letters patent 1565; see p. 27.
23 TNA, C 142/209/21.
24 Hockaday Abs.; GDR vol. 2A, 151; see p. 68.
25 Hockaday Abs.; GDR vol. 27A, 27.
26 *Eccl. Misc.* 86; GA, D 1923, bundle 13, 'Bainhams' d. 1638.
27 GA, MF 1182, ff. 47–51 (GDR Gen. Act Book); TNA, PROB 11/304/343.
28 GDR vol. 282A; ibid. 284; http://www.theclergydatabase.org.uk (accessed 28 Jan. 2015).
29 *Benson's Surv.* 39; TNA, PROB 11/304/343.
30 GDR, D 5/3/39.
31 Ibid.; GDR vol. 319A; Hockaday Abs.
32 GDR vol. 333; GDR, D 5/3/39; Hockaday Abs.; TNA, IR 18/2952.
33 GDR vol. 358; GDR, D 5/3/39; Hockaday Abs.
34 GDR, D 5/3/39.

Emmott (d. 1917) and then his widow, were lay patrons until the advowson was conveyed to the bishop of Gloucester in 1926–7.[35]

Income and Endowment

In 1291 the rectory was valued at £13 6s 8d,[36] and this increased to a value 'not exceeding 60 marks' (£40) in 1411.[37] In c.1535 the total value of the rectory and tithe was calculated at £30 18s.[38] This remained largely unchanged c.1690 and in 1750.[39]

During the 13th century the church of Yate asserted its right to the tithes of Itchington, a tithing of Tytherington parish, which also lay within Hawkesbury deanery. In 1275 the bishop of Worcester established a commission to settle a dispute between Yate's rector, Thomas of Gloucester, and Robert de Wych, rector of Tytherington, respecting Thomas's claim to the tithes of Itchington and another field called Bockney near Wickwar.[40] No outcome was recorded, but this may account for the inclusion of 'the tithes and living of Yate' in the valuation of Tytherington in 1291.[41]

The rector of Yate received both great and small tithes at the end of the 16th century. A modus or agreement of 1584 between the rector, Thomas Baynham, and the parishioners formalised the 'ancient' parochial custom of monetary payments in lieu of tithes in kind.[42] This stipulated that payments were due for cattle, sheep, pigs and geese, and 2d. for every load of hay; but tithes of wool, eggs, honey and corn were still to be paid in kind. Hay cut in Hallmead, Northmead and Duckmead were tithe free, in recognition of an allotment to the parson of a meadow called Nine Acres.

This agreement applied predominantly to the manor of Yate; tenants of Brinsham were still liable for tithes of hay from the otherwise exempted fields, and the modus did not apply to Stanshawes manor, nor to Wapley and Codrington parishes, which still owed tithes to the rector of Yate.[43] In Stanshawes the arrangements for paying tithes on cattle, sheep, pigs and hay varied, and appear to have been negotiated between the rector and individual tenants.[44] Cases laid before the ecclesiastical courts at Gloucester suggest that these transactions were not straightforward. In c.1600 Robert Yewen argued that the customary payments he had been making were too high, and thereafter paid his tithes in kind. In 1604 David Jordan, a tenant of Stanshawes, was also in dispute with Baynham regarding his payments.[45] The cause of an earlier dispute, which resulted in the bishop of Gloucester petitioning the crown for Henry Stanshawe to be imprisoned, is unknown, but may have involved tithe payments. He had been excommunicated in 1594 for his contumacy in not appearing to answer the charges of the rector, Thomas Baynham.[46]

35   GDR, D 5/3/39.
36   *Tax. Eccl.*
37   *Cal. Pap. Reg.* VI, 206.
38   *Valor Eccl.* II, 491.
39   *Parsons's Notes*, 289; *Benson's Surv.* 39.
40   *Reg. Giffard* I, 77, 81.
41   *Tax. Eccl.* sig. Tytherington, 220.
42   This para, GA, D 9125/2/6742, dated 1584.
43   Ibid.; GDR vol. 89, 395.
44   GDR vol. 89, 395.
45   Ibid.
46   Hockaday Abs.

These complex arrangements continued to frustrate the payment of Yate's tithes in the 18th century, and hindered the process of commutation in the early 19th century. Between 1709 and 1720 the rector, William Mason, entered several causes against Robert Oxwick, lord of Yate manor, for refusing to pay the small tithes in kind for Yate Court farm.[47] Oxwick claimed he had offered the rector adequate payment according to the terms of the 1584 modus but it had been refused; Mason successfully argued that the modus did not apply to Court farm, citing his defeat of a similar case made by the farm's former tenant, John Symonds, in 1709. Oxwick's subsequent appeal to the House of Lords was rejected; he was required to pay Mason's costs, and the order for tithes to be paid in kind was upheld.[48] The report on Yate to the Tithe Commissioners in 1838 observed that an attempt had been made 'many years ago to establish a modus which after much lengthened litigation . . . was found could not be maintained.'[49] Despite this, in 1841 Daniel Shipp, tenant of Tanhouse farm (adjacent to Yate Court), objected to the proposed tithe rent charge for his holding, 'Hayleaze', on the grounds that it was part of Northmead and therefore exempt from tithes of hay.[50]

Between 1820 and 1835 the tithes were worth on average £630 yearly. Despite several abatements, arrears of £300–400 were still owed to the rector for the same period. At commutation in 1841, the rent charge was set at £685.[51] In 1869 it had increased to £717 10s, with an additional £9 paid on land in Wapley and Codrington.[52]

In 1635 Yate rectory possessed 13 parcels of glebe land, totalling about 60 a.; most were let as two holdings for the sum of £60.[53] From at least 1584 the glebe had included a lodge and glebe house in addition to the parsonage.[54] Two dwellings were also recorded in 1704, by when at least four more parcels had been added to the glebe lands.[55] In 1743 the rectory manor comprised c.200 a.[56] The glebe covered c.152 a. in 1841, and slightly more than 162 a. in 1869.[57] By then most of the glebe was let as two farms and three smaller allotments, of which two were copyholds under the rectory manor. The larger of the two farms, latterly known as Rectory farm, extended over 114 a. north of the church and rectory, and either side of Church Lane.[58]

The lands attached to Rectory farm contained celestine. Both Alfred Pontifex and his successor as rector, James Madden Ford, allowed local speculators, including C. Pauli (latterly of Yate Mineral and Land Co.) to work the glebe for the mineral. In 1900 Ford leased the strontia on the glebe to Sydney Gunning and Frank Cox for a maximum

47   This para, R. Oxwick and E. Simpsion, Oxwick *and Simpsion, Appellants; Mason, Respondent. The Appellants' Case* (1720); R. Oxwick and E. Simpsion, *R. Oxwick ... and E. Simpsion, his Tenant, Appellants; W. Mason, ... Respondent. The Respondent's Case* (1720); BL General Ref. Colln. 19.h.1. (103) and (104).
48   *LJ*, 20, 205 (23 Jan. 1720).
49   TNA, IR 18/2952.
50   Ibid.; GA, D 9125/2/6742, dated 1584.
51   TNA, IR 18/2952.
52   GDR, D 5/3/39.
53   GDR, V 5/356 T2.
54   GDR, V 5/356 T1.
55   GDR, V 5/356 T6.
56   GDR, D 5/3/39.
57   GDR, T 1/207; ibid. D 5/3/39.
58   GDR, D 5/3/39; MA 75; GDR, T 1/207; OS Map 25", Glos. LXIX.6 (1882 edn).

Figure 21 *The late Georgian rectory, c.1910.*

annual rent of £20 plus royalties on the amounts raised.[59] In 1907 Rectory farm was sold to Cox.[60]

By 1921 most of the remaining glebe land had been sold,[61] so that from 1926 until 1948 the rectory retained only 4 or 5 a.[62] Between 1870 and *c.*1960 the total annual income of the living remained at around £1,000, with the provision of a residence.[63]

A parsonage house at Yate was recorded in a terrier of 1584,[64] and the survey of 1635 suggests that it was located north of the church.[65] A substantial house, approximately 200 m. north-east of the church, had replaced this early dwelling by 1824;[66] it may have occupied the same site, since earlier outbuildings remained.[67] The rectory grounds were bounded by the river Frome to the south and Church Lane to the east.[68] A terraced garden extended south-west from the house to the river, which was crossed by a small

59   BRO P. St MY/I/4 (b); see pp. 50–3.
60   GDR, D 5/3/39.
61   BRO, P St MY/I/5 Eccl. Comm. Inquiry, 1921.
62   *Crockford's Clerical Dir.* (1926, 1948 edns).
63   *Crockford's Clerical Dir.* (1870, 1948, 1930, 1961–2 edns).
64   GDR, V 5/356 T1
65   GDR, V 5/356 T4
66   Greenwood, *Map of Glos.* (1824); OS Map 25", Glos. LXIX.6 (1882 edn); YHC, Murray Dowding Collection, Yate Rectory *c.*1910.
67   YHC, Murray Dowding Collection; http://www.parksandgardens.org, record 7071 (accessed Dec. 2013).
68   Greenwood, *Map of Glos.* (1824); OS Map 25", Glos. LXIX.6 (1882 edn).

wooden bridge;[69] a tree-lined avenue connected the rectory to the church.[70] The rectory house was extensive, including nine bedrooms and four reception rooms. In 1921, the rector, James Madden Ford, described it as an unsuitable residence, being 'much too large and expensive'.[71] It was sold in 1926 and replaced in 1928 by a new house, built on the plot of land immediately north of the old site.[72] Rectory Farm and the late Georgian rectory house were demolished to make way for extensive residential development between 1970 and 1989.[73] The incumbent's residence was relocated to Canterbury Close, which had been built in the 1980s on the site of the former rectory.[74]

Religious Life

The Medieval Period

The parish church underwent substantial development between the 14th and 16th centuries.[75] It is likely that the Norman church was replaced during the 13th century by one of cruciform plan; remnants of Early English work are evident in the smaller arches and pillars at the western end of the nave, and 12th-century stone was re-used in the porch at the south entrance. The chancel, north and south chapels, the nave north and east walls, and the west tower, were all built or rebuilt in Perpendicular style. The tower of *c.*1500 incorporated the Tudor rose motif in its decoration, perhaps in honour of Henry VII. There is evidence of a collapsed central tower that necessitated the rebuilding of the eastern portion of the nave in the mid 16th century, accounting for the stylistic differences in the two eastern bays of the north arcade. The majority of the windows were also Perpendicular; although most stained glass was replaced in the late 19th century,[76] one window in the north-east corner of the north chancel retained fragments of patterned medieval glass.[77]

Considerable investment was made during this period to the church interior. The second, third and fourth bells of the ring of six were the product of Bristol foundries between 1450 and 1500, the third commissioned by Robert Stanshawe.[78] In 1514 John Benham, former rector of Yate, bequeathed £10, 'to the payntyng and gyldyng of the chauncell and the roode lofte'.[79] A medieval painting of St Christopher with a watermill was visible in 2014 on the nave north wall.[80] The octagonal font with panelled stem, also

69   OS Map 25", Glos. LXIX.6 (1882 edn); http://www.parksandgardens.org, record 7071 (accessed Dec. 2013).

70   OS Map 25", Glos. LXIX.6 (1882 edn).

71   BRO, P St MY/I/5 Eccl. Comm. Inquiry, 1921.

72   BRO, P St MY/I/5 Old and New Residence Account, 1930; OS Map 25", ST7182 (1951 edn).

73   HER S. Glos. no. 2911; OS1970 and 1989, 1:10000, ST78SW.

74   Diocese of Bristol, *Yate New Town Parish Profile* (2012–13); OS1989, 1:10000, ST78SW.

75   This para, Verey and Brooks, *Glos.* II, 824; NHL, no. 1128753, Parish Church of St Mary the Virgin: 12 Feb. 2015; *Trans. BGAS*, 13 (1888) 2; site visit, 2013.

76   See pp. 100–1.

77   F. Walter, *The History of Yate Church* (*c.*1997).

78   H.B. Walters, 'Church bells of Glos.', *Trans. BGAS*, 18 (1893–4), 240–50; ibid., 41 (1918), 73.

79   TNA, PROB 11/18/69.

80   Site visit, 2013; HER S. Glos. no. 2084.

in situ in 2014, dates from *c.*1500.[81] Two scratch dials and a mass dial with an angel above the priest's door also survived.[82]

Although a complete account of the incumbency of the church at Yate cannot be established for the medieval period, 12 rectors were recorded by name for the period 1271–1522.[83]

Table 8 *Rectors, 1271–1522*

1271	Thomas of Gloucester	1391	Edward Dauntsey
1311	Reginald de Willington	1402	Roger Smyth
1319	Robert de Willington	1406	Henry Gardiner
1342	Thomas de Weston in Gordano	1432	Thomas Shepey
1348	Robert Ewyas	*c.*1514	John Benham
1358	Roger Yonge	1522	Edward Sheffield

During his lordship of the manor of Yate, John de Willington (I) sought to present members of his own family.[84] In 1311 he presented his younger brother Reginald to the living.[85] Weeks after his institution, Reginald was granted leave of absence to complete his studies.[86] During his absence a writ for arrears of 26*s.* 8*d.* to a royal subsidy was issued by the sheriff against Yate church.[87] Reginald had quit the living by 1319, and Robert de Willington was instituted as rector; his exact relationship to his patron is unclear, but when appointed he was living in London.[88]

Several of Yate's medieval incumbents augmented their income by holding multiple benefices. Edward Dauntsey, bachelor of canon and civil laws from Salisbury diocese,[89] was instituted rector in 1392 by Sir Thomas West,[90] who held the advowson by right of his marriage to Joan, Ralph de Willington's widow.[91] Dauntsey was almost immediately absent from the parish, having been granted a licence of non-residence for two years.[92] In 1397 he was collated archdeacon of Cornwall, with an annexed prebend in Glasney collegiate church (also Cornw.); and in 1402 he exchanged his living at Yate with Roger Smyth, prebendary of St Probus (Cornw.).[93] Smyth likewise exchanged in 1406 with Henry Gardiner,[94] who also held the canonry and prebend of Taunton (Bath & Wells diocese), and Blaenporth (Cards.) and Llansantffraid (Cards.) both in St David's diocese. In 1411 he was granted further dispensation to hold one other benefice or cure for two

---

81   Verey and Brooks, *Glos.* II, 825; site visit, 2013.
82   Site visit, 2013.
83   Bps Regs. Worcs; Bp. Reg. Stafford (Exeter Dioc); Hockaday Abs. Yate (re 1271, 1391, 1402).
84   See pp. 90–2.
85   *Reg. Reynolds* 88.
86   Ibid., 152.
87   Ibid., 172.
88   *Reg. Cobham* 231.
89   *Cal. Papal Reg.* IV, 497.
90   *Reg. Wakefeld,* 102.
91   Burke, *Visitation of the Seats and Arms of the Noblemen and Gentlemen of Great Britain* (1852) I, 268.
92   *Reg. Wakefeld,* 119.
93   F.C. Hingeston Randolph, *Reg. of Edm. Stafford* (1886), 80.
94   Ibid., 110.

years.[95] Whether Gardiner resided at Yate is unclear, but at his death in 1419 he was recorded as vicar of Blackawton (Devon).[96] A later pluralist was Edward Sheffield, who held Yate from 1522 with the vicarage of Luton (Beds.) to which he was presented in 1502. The brass dedicated to his memory in St Mary's Church, Luton, cites him as rector of Camborne (Cornw.), and a prebendary of Lichfield cathedral.[97]

From Reformation to Restoration, c.1530–1660

Early resistance to the break with Rome was apparent among some of Yate's more prominent residents. In 1536, John Barlow, dean of Westbury college, complained to Thomas Cromwell of threats made against him by Anne, Lady Berkeley, then lessee of Yate Court. A dispute had arisen after Barlow witnessed a tennis match played in Yate during morning service. He alleged that when Lady Berkeley discovered his intention to prosecute the offenders, she abused him publicly, wishing he had been beaten and threatening that 'she would sit upon [his] skirts'. He further claimed that she had purchased the next gaol delivery (endeavoured to determine the fate of defendents by paying the equivalent of fines owed to the court to the crown), and pursued various causes against him. One charge stemmed from an earlier dispute: in 1535 Barlow and Sir Nicholas Poyntz (the Berkeleys' neighbour at Acton Court) had attempted to seize William Norton, a priest, 'for the keeping of certain prohibited books', notably Bishop Fisher's work for the 'maintenance of the said Bishop of Rome'; Lady Berkeley had been accused of protecting Norton.[98]

Despite this extraordinary case, little upheaval was discernible among the parish's clergy in the early phases of the reformation. In 1544 John France served the cure of Yate,[99] and in 1548 a Dr Bowlam was recorded as rector, with John Glover as his curate.[100] At Bishop Hooper's visitation in 1551 Dr Bowlam remained the incumbent, but did not reside. In his absence his curate, Patrick Durye, was assessed; he could repeat the articles of faith and the Lord's Prayer, and could locate, but not recite, the Ten Commandments.[101]

George Morris succeeded Bowlam on his death in 1552.[102] He resided in the parish in 1561 and 1563, had no curate and preached in the church himself.[103] He refused, however, to conform to aspects of new policy under Elizabethan protestantism, and in 1572 was deprived of his living for not reading the articles.[104]

Further evidence of reaction to the Reformation in the parish is ambiguous, as deficiencies in particular church goods may indicate resistance. In 1569 the diocesan

95   *Cal. Papal Reg.* VI, 206.
96   Randolph, *Reg. of Edm. Stafford*, 147.
97   *Testamenta Eboracensia* IV (1869), 120.
98   *L & P Hen. VIII*, XI, Nov. 1536; Hockaday Abs Yate; C. Litzenberger, *English Reformation and the Laity: Glos. 1540–1580* (2002), 37–8.
99   http://theclergydatabase.org.uk (accessed 28 Jan. 2015).
100 GDR vol. 4; http://theclergydatabase.org.uk (accessed 28 Jan. 2015).
101 J. Gairdner, 'Bishop Hooper's Visitation of Gloucester', *EHR* 19 (1904), 116.
102 Worcs. RO, b 716.093–BA.2648/9b(iv) episcopal register; http://theclergydatabase.org.uk (accessed 28 Jan. 2015).
103 http://theclergydatabase.org.uk (accessed 28 Jan. 2015); GA, D 6755/2/2, 17.
104 GDR vol. 27a, 27.

consistory court ordered that a surplice be provided, and in 1572 the churchwardens reported that they lacked a communion cup (replacing the chalice associated with Catholic mass).[105] However, these defects may reflect the expense of changing liturgical practice rather than opposition to it. Bequests to the parish church declined from 1544, and reports in 1563, 1569 and 1572 confirmed that the church windows and the churchyard were in a state of disrepair.[106] Similarly, it is unclear whether personal disputes underlay the excommunication of three parishioners for giving a 'blowe in the churche yard' shortly after the deprivation of Morris, or whether their appearance before the ecclesiastical courts signalled dissent from the newly established church.[107]

Morris's successors were certainly more inclined to conform. Thomas Baynham, who was instituted on his predecessor's deprivation, remained as rector of Yate for 50 years. In the diocesan survey of 1603 he was listed as a public preacher, and his already valuable living at Yate was augmented by the nearby rectory of Frampton Cotterell.[108] One of Baynham's patrons, Thomas Neale, was the father of a Hebrew scholar (also Thomas) highly praised by Queen Elizabeth for his gift to her in 1566 of Latin verses.[109] William Hutchinson was rector from 1622 until his death in 1660;[110] in 1623, shortly after his institution, Thomas Hughes was licensed as curate, and Richard Godwyn in 1635.[111] In 1639 Hutchinson was admitted to the office of rural dean of Hawkesbury.[112] Despite clerical continuity, however, presentments made between 1594 and 1638 for negligent attendance at church and failure to receive communion, suggest continued resistance among the laity.[113]

The Re-established Church and Nonconformity, c.1660–1840

Between 1660 and 1843 Yate had six rectors; most were pluralists who entrusted the parish to a curate. Jeremiah Horler, rector between 1660 and 1685,[114] employed Thomas Skinner as his curate in 1669.[115] Horler, following his predecessor Hutchinson, also served as rural dean of Hawkesbury from 1684.[116] Francis Gold, curate in 1735 during the incumbency of William Mason (1686–1740),[117] had strong local connections, having been a schoolteacher at Chipping Sodbury; he left Yate after Mason's death to take up the vicarage of Wapley with Codrington.[118] Samuel Seyer was appointed assistant curate in 1741, shortly after the institution of Richard Wallington as rector.[119] Seyer was also

105 GDR vol. 26, 17; ibid., 29, 123; Litzenberger, *English Reformation*, 131–4.
106 Hockaday Abs. Yate; GDR vol. 26, 17; ibid., 29, 123.
107 GDR vol. 29; Hockaday Abs. Yate; W. Cobbett, *Cobbett's Legacy to Parsons* (1835), 53.
108 *Eccl. Misc.* 65, 281.
109 MS Bodl. 13 part 1 T. Neale (1566); J.A. Neale, *Charters and Records of the Neales of Berkeley, Yate and Corsham* (1906), 16, 21, 167.
110 Hock. Abs. Yate; GDR vols. 185 and 142A, 48.
111 GDR vols. 146, 185.
112 GDR vol. 142; http://theclergydatabase.org.uk (accessed 28 Jan. 2015).
113 GDR vols. 76, 116, 137, 138; GA, D 2052/1, Yate.
114 GA, MF 1182 (GDR Gen. Act Book); GDR vol. 248, 31.
115 GDR vol. 208, p. 175; Hockaday Abs.
116 GDR vol. 249a; http://theclergydatabase.org.uk (accessed 28 Jan. 2015).
117 *Benson's Surv.* 39; GDR vols. 248, 284; Hockaday Abs.
118 http://theclergydatabase.org.uk (accessed 28 Jan. 2015).
119 GDR vols. 282a, 284.

licensed to Horsley, a parish more than 15 miles north of Yate, where Wallington held the vicarage.[120] Thomas Tournay, rector 1765–95, was another pluralist; besides Yate he held two livings in Kent, as vicar of Hougham and rector of St James's, Dover,[121] and seems to have been absent from Yate from at least 1791.[122] Tournay's curate, Richard John Hay, purchased the advowson and rectory manor in 1791, and was instituted as rector on his predecessor's death in 1795. Hay left his parish in 1796 and resigned the living in 1801;[123] his curate, William Stephen Goodenough, was instituted as rector in the same year.[124] Although Goodenough held no other office, in 1842, shortly before he died the following year,[125] he nominated William Philip Haselwood as curate,[126] for an annual stipend of £100, on condition that he resided within the parish.[127] A stipendiary curate was subsequently retained at Yate until the end of the 19th century.[128]

The periodic absence of the incumbents of Yate may have contributed to the growth of nonconformist worship within the parish from the second half of the 17th century. In 1676 there were 250 conformists recorded at Yate, compared to seven nonconformists and no papists.[129] The dissenters included at least two Quakers, John Neale and William Sturge, who featured prominently in presentments made for non-attendance between 1676 and 1684.[130] They were excommunicated along with 'all dissidents from the parish church' in 1678.[131] No monthly meeting was established within the parish, but from the early 18th century some of Yate's Quakers attended the Sodbury meeting house, formally certified in 1690.[132] Earlier marriages from 1665 and 1679 indicate that residents of Yate may also have frequented meetings at Frenchay and Olveston.[133]

The nonconformist branch of the Neales resident at Yate were members of a well-established south Gloucestershire family and freeholders of the parish.[134] From the end of the 17th century Robert Neale enjoyed an uneasy relationship with the rector, William Mason, who pursued him for non-payment of tithes with a determination similar to that applied in his cause against Robert Oxwick.[135] In 1678 and 1691 Neale was committed to prison in contempt of the rector and the chancellor of the diocese. On a near annual basis between 1693 and 1701 the rector's servants entered Neale's property and forcibly took what was owed; in 1694 it was noted that they 'hoved [the gate] off the hooks'

120 http://theclergydatabase.org.uk (accessed 28 Jan. 2015); GDR vol. 282A.
121 http://theclergydatabase.org.uk (accessed 28 Jan. 2015); TNA, PROB 11/1258/232; E. Hasted, *Hist. and Topography of Kent* (2nd edn, 1800) IX, 451–62, n. 11.
122 GDR, D 5/3/39.
123 GDR, D 5/3/39; GDR vol. 319A.
124 GDR vol. 319A, 303–5; see p. 91.
125 TNA, PROB 11/1977, f.368v.
126 GDR vol. 362, 53.
127 GDR vol. 358, 355.
128 GDR vol. 385 Survey 1864 x 1869.
129 *Compton Census*, 536.
130 TNA, RG 6/1359; GA, D 2052/1; GDR vols. 227, 231, 233, 243, 255.
131 GDR vol. 233.
132 TNA, RG 31/6; ibid. RG 6/1443; GA, D 2052/1.
133 TNA, RG 6/1359, 1366.
134 Neale, *Charters*, 76; see p. 27.
135 GA, D 2052/1; see pp. 69, 93.

in order to gain entry.[136] Between 1795 and 1817, Toby Walker Sturge, a Quaker and gentleman of the parish, was likewise delinquent in his annual tithe payments to the rector, from 1801 William Goodenough.[137]

Other dissenting congregations formed within the parish from the end of the 17th century. The house of William Pullen was certified by Anabaptists in 1699,[138] and by c.1717 there was a Presbyterian chapel serving Yate and Wickwar, with a local congregation of 150 hearers under the ministry of Rice Griffiths.[139] Surveys of 1735, 1740, and 1750 saw little change in Yate's religious community; from a parish population of 320, five Quakers, or one Quaker family, and 15 Presbyterians were recorded.[140] From the beginning of the 19th century a Baptist cause emerged in the parish. The houses of James Chambers and Mrs Alpass, both in Yate, were certified in 1817 by Esra Horlick, Baptist minister of Chipping Sodbury, as places of worship; and in 1819 William Southwood, also a Baptist minister of Chipping Sodbury, certified for worship a room in Rebecca Shipp's premises.[141] In 1841 the Baptist Meeting Society owned 4 a. of land on the eastern parish boundary near Yate Rocks for use as a meeting ground.[142]

From 1840 to 1950

The parish church underwent substantial alterations during the second half of the 19th century. In 1859 the nave was renovated by public subscription, including the replacement of the pews.[143] In 1879 the rector, Alfred Pontifex, restored the chancel at a cost of £2,228.[144] The stained glass east window above the altar, to a design informed by the work of the German Renaissance artist Albrecht Dürer, was dedicated to the memory of Alfred's father, Edmund Pontifex.[145]

A faculty to restore the church exterior was obtained in 1897.[146] Initially, the building committee intended to complete the church tower as a diamond jubilee celebration, but the dilapidated state of much of the church structure required new windows, porch and ceiling timbers.[147] Francis Fox of Yate House chaired the committee and the treasurer was Gathorne Hill. They retained a noted church architect, W.D. Caröe, to complete the restoration work;[148] he had also re-built Poole Court for Hill before 1884.[149] The committee had raised £2,728 towards the estimated cost of £2,820 by 1900, through donations from the parish's chief landholders, former rectors and local businesses, and

136 GA, D 2052/1.
137 Ibid.; TNA, RG 6/1443, f. 6; ibid. PROB 11/1954/204.
138 TNA, RG 31/6 f. 73.
139 T.S. James, *History of the Litigation and Legislation respecting the Presbyterian chapels of England and Wales, between 1816 and 1849* (1867), 661; GA, Q/SO/4/3.
140 GDR vols. 285B, 397, 381B.
141 GDR vol. 334B, 290–1.
142 GDR, T 1/207.
143 BRO P. St MY/ChW/1; *Kelly's Dir. Glos.* (1879 edn), 793.
144 *Kelly's Dir. Glos.* (1894 edn), 358; ibid. (1906 edn), 371.
145 GA, A 98/15959GS; site visit, 2013.
146 BRO, P St MY/ChW/1.
147 BRO, P St MY/ChW/2.
148 Ibid.
149 Verey and Brooks, *Glos.* II, 828; see pp. 18, 65 fig. 2.

Figure 22 *St Mary's Church tower, restored 1897–1900, and the memorial lychgate (1921), designed by W.D. Caröe.*

from fundraising sales and bazaars.[150] By 1910 the tower was completed with a crown of buttressed pinnacles, the porch and ceiling had been restored, and new stained glass windows installed in the north and south chancel walls.[151] The total cost was believed to exceed £3,000.[152]

150 BRO, P St MY/ChW/2.
151 GA, A 98/15959GS; site visit, 2013; F. Ashley, *The History of Yate Church*, 5–10.
152 *Kelly's Dir. Glos.* (1906 edn), 371.

Figure 23 *The chancel window after Albrecht Dürer, installed by Alfred Pontifex, rector 1869–96.*

A memorial lychgate, also designed by Caröe, was unveiled in 1921, with a procession of ex-servicemen and the families of fallen men;[153] additions to the memorial were made in 1947 after the Second World War.[154]

The early restoration work took place during the incumbencies of George Ludford Harvey and Alfred Pontifex. Harvey, instituted to the living in 1843,[155] was the son of Sir Ludford Harvey, a former vice-president of the Royal College of Surgeons, and had previously served as curate of Bitton and vicar of Diseworth (Leics.), and as a chaplain to the duke of York.[156] A new window inserted in the north chapel in its north wall

153 YHC, D/215 A; Verey and Brooks, *Glos*. II, 826.
154 BRO, P St MY/ChW/1.
155 GDR vol. 351, 226; Hockaday Abs.
156 *Ann. Reg.* 71 (1830), 249; *Gents. Mag.* 92, 2 (1822), 87; *Alumni Cantab*. II, 276.

commemorated his tenure.[157] Alfred Pontifex, previously curate of Little Cheverell
(Wilts.),[158] succeeded Harvey as rector in 1869. Aside from his investment in the fabric
of the church, Pontifex was active locally as a strontia speculator and as the chaplain of
the masonic lodge at Chipping Sodbury.[159] During six months' absence in 1873 through
poor health, he delegated his parish duties to his curate, James Westcourt Douglas, who
lived in the parish at the glebe house.[160] Despite resigning the living in 1896, Pontifex
retained a connection with the local community; his son Percy, a naval officer, who had
been born at the rectory, was buried in the 'family vault' at Yate church in 1908. Many
villagers attended his funeral, at which Pontifex's successor, James Madden Ford (rector
1896–1922), officiated.[161]

Five rectors served the parish between 1922 and 1961. Herbert Forster Morris,
formerly curate of Walcot in Bath,[162] resigned the living in 1930 after eight years and was
replaced by Edward Frederick Smith,[163] who committed suicide in 1933. It was reported
that he feared his financial difficulties would bring disgrace on the church,[164] and that
these resulted from problems encountered after his wife's death, when he was vicar of
Tewkesbury.[165] Some also considered that his predicament stemmed from excessive
generosity to his parishioners.[166] His replacement, Jerome Alexander Bass Mercier, rector
of Kemerton from 1902,[167] was collated to the rectory of Yate in November 1933.[168] In
1948 Lawrence Victor Wraith, vicar of Coleford with Staunton and honorary chaplain to
the bishop of Gloucester, succeeded Mercer as rector of Yate. Wraith was well placed to
oversee the emerging urban parish, as he had begun his clerical career in Manchester.[169]

In 1851 morning and afternoon services were held at St Mary's church, with average
attendance of 120 and 200 respectively. The rector remarked that few parishioners
attended both services on account of distance from the church. There were also 100
Sunday school scholars.[170] In 1855 a church-sponsored National School for boys and girls
was built immediately south of the churchyard.[171] The church also supported a parish
branch of the Mother's Union, established before 1929,[172] and in 1934 a parish hall was
erected on Station Road.[173] In c.1948 the church choir comprised 14 boys, eight women
and 12 men.[174]

157 Site visit, 2013; F. Ashley, *A History of Yate Church*, 7.
158 *Hants. Advertiser,* 30 Sept. 1865.
159 See p. 93; *Era,* 16 Nov. 1873.
160 GDR vol. 376, 116; *Crockford's Clerical Dir.* (1896); Hockaday Abs.
161 *Bath Chronicle,* 11 June 1908; *Crockford's Clerical Dir.* (1921–2).
162 *Bath Chronicle* Sept. 1922; *Crockford's Clerical Dir.* (1926, 1927).
163 *Citizen,* 13 June 1930; *Crockford's Clerical Dir.* (1932).
164 *Western Daily Press,* 29 Mar. 1933.
165 Ibid.; *Western Daily Press,* 2 Apr. 1930.
166 *Western Daily Press,* 29 Mar. 1933.
167 *Citizen,* 13 Sept. 1902.
168 *Western Daily Press,* 11 and 13 Nov. 1933; *Crockford's Clerical Dir.* (1948).
169 *Citizen,* 15 Sept 1948; *Crockford's Clerical Dir.* (1961–2).
170 TNA, HO 129/331, religious census 1851, f. 47.
171 TNA, ED 103/26/34; NHL, no. 1128752, Youth Centre, 35yd. s. of St Mary's Ch.: 12 Feb. 2015; see
     pp.80–3.
172 See pp. 85–6.
173 *Kelly's Dir. Glos.* (1939 edn), 389; Verey and Brooks, *Glos.* II, 826.
174 YHC, D/250/2.

Figure 24 *The Baptist chapel on North Road, c.1910.*

Although no nonconformist churches were recorded in 1851, Baptist, Wesleyan and Congregational chapels had been established in the parish before 1879.[175] A Brethren chapel, later referred to as the Gospel Hall, was built west of the junction of Station Road and Church Road in 1862.[176] Before the chapel opened, members met in a local cottage. In 1922 plans were made to establish a Sunday school and restart a weekly evening meeting for young people.[177] In 1961 it was acknowledged that the Gospel Hall might have to be removed because of the new town development, and it closed in 1969.[178]

A Baptist chapel with 50 sittings was established some distance from the village centre at Yate Rocks in 1881. Served from Wickwar, there were ten members at Yate in 1896, four Sunday school teachers and 36 scholars.[179] A second chapel was opened on North Road, serving the colliery community in the west of the parish in 1909.[180]

A branch of the Wesleyan Methodist church met at Yate in temporary premises until the construction of a chapel on Station Road.[181] The new building to seat 100 was

175   Religious Census 1851, f. 47; *Kelly's Dir. Glos.* (1897 edn), 367–8.
176   *Kelly's Dir. Glos.* (1894 edn), 358; OS Map 6", Glos. LXIX.SW (1903 edn); OS 1955, 1:10000, ST78SW.
177   YHC 94001/1, minute book.
178   Ibid.; *London Gazette* 3 May 1969, 5027.
179   Baptist Union, *Baptist Chapel Handbook* (1896), 217.
180   YHC, H. Lane, notes on non-conformity; date on plaque at site.
181   *Kelly's Dir. Glos.* (1879 edn); YHC, Thornbury Wesleyan Circuit Yate Scheme, 1904.

erected in 1905,[182] but closed when the chapel moved to Moorland Road in 1941.[183] The congregation continued to meet there in 2014.[184]

A Christian Science chapel was recorded on Stover Road in 1939.[185] The Christadelphians, who had met within the parish from 1920, opened a hall on North Road in 1953, which was still in use in 2014.[186]

The New Town Parish

The growth of the urban area in Yate resulted in changes to the form and function of the churches within the parish. From *c.*1977 a team of clergy comprising the rector, two vicars and a curate, served the newly constituted 'new town parish'.[187] St Mary's church was re-ordered to make it 'a centre of Christian activity'.[188] Robert Parker, rector between 1974 and 1981, defended the proposed changes. He emphasised the need for the church to reflect 'present day economic and changing theological attitudes', to facilitate community activities as well as worship.[189] Parker had already been responsible for planning a cross-denominational programme of free training for the unemployed youth of the new town in 1975.[190] Despite some local opposition the alterations to the church were completed in 1979. An extension containing a kitchen and utilities was added to the nave north wall, and the pews were removed and replaced with chairs. The base of the tower was converted into the church offices, funded by a donation from Newman Electrical Motors. A plain glass window was installed above the office doors, engraved with an acknowledgement of the donation and the image of Alexander Staples and his family derived from a church brass of *c.*1590.[191] Further work to level and carpet the floor of the church was undertaken in 1997.[192]

To serve the new community of south Yate, a second Anglican church was opened in Abbotswood in 1978. St Nicholas's church or St Nicholas family centre was constructed as an extension of the youth centre built in 1969.[193] In 2012–13 the family centre provided special worship services for children and young families and a Sunday morning youth group, in addition to facilities in the youth centre. St Mary's church continued to host Yate Mothers' Union and a community craft group, as well as holding regular services. The new town parish was served by two full-time stipendiary clergy, the team rector and team vicar, who were assisted by four lay preachers and an associate minister.[194]

The new town development also stimulated the growth of a Catholic community at Yate. Served by the church of St Lawrence, which had been established at Chipping

182 *Kelly's Dir. Glos.* (1906 edn), 371.
183 *London Gazette*, 30 Sept. 1941, p. 5679.
184 http://www.yatemethodist.co.uk (accessed 28 Jan. 2015).
185 *Kelly's Dir. Glos.* (1939 edn), 389.
186 http://www.ukchristadelphians.org.uk (accessed 30 Jan. 2015).
187 *Crockford's Clerical Dir.* (1977–9).
188 YHC, *Gazette* 15 Jan. 1977.
189 Ibid.
190 *Catholic Herald*, 31 Oct. 1975.
191 *Gazette* 15 Jan. 1977; F. Ashley, *A History of Yate Church*, 5; site visit, 2013.
192 Diocese of Bristol, *Yate Parish Profile* 2012.
193 Ibid.; Verey and Brooks, *Glos.* II, 826.
194 Diocese of Bristol: *Yate Parish Profile* 2012; site visit, 2013.

Sodbury in 1838, mass was held at Yate parish hall from 1965, and at Rodford junior school from 1972.[195] St Paul's Catholic primary school, situated just west of Stanshawes Court, was opened in 1974, and served as a mass centre until 1981. In 1979 plans were agreed to build a church at Yate, resulting in St Paul's, opened by the bishop of Clifton, Mervyn Alexander, in 1981.[196] In 2014 the Catholic communities at Yate and Chipping Sodbury belonged to the parish of St Lawrence and St Paul, in the diocese of Clifton.[197]

Table 9 *Religious denominations, Yate 2001–11*

	2001	*2011*
Christian	16,027	12,797
Buddhist	17	41
Hindu	25	25
Jewish	8	4
Muslim	63	73
Sikh	9	22
Other religion	46	99
No religion	3,963	6,963
Not stated	1,628	1,579
Total population	*21,786*	*21,603*

From 2001 increasing numbers of non-Christian individuals were recorded among Yate's population, reflecting the growing diversity of the urban area.[198] The permanent places of worship established within the parish remained exclusively Christian, however, and Bristol provided the nearest non-Christian centres.[199]

195   E. Murphy, *History of St Lawrence's Parish, Chipping Sodbury* (1988), 20, 29–32.
196   Ibid.; *London Gazette*, 22 Oct. 1981, p. 13403; see p. 83.
197   http://www.cliftondiocese.com (accessed 28 Jan. 2015).
198   *Census*, 2001, 2011.
199   S. Glos. Council: parish profile, 2005–14.

SOURCES AND ABBREVIATIONS

THIS VCH HISTORY OF YATE has been written using a wide range of sources, including original archives, published editions of documents, printed material, online resources, oral reminiscences, ephemera, maps and images. Wherever possible the text is supported by primary sources, created at the time of, and as part of, the processes and events they describe, and details are given in the footnotes. These are necessarily abbreviated, and a list of the most common abbreviations is given below. Full details of others, used only occasionally in this history, will be found prefaced to published volumes in the VCH Gloucestershire series. Most original documents have been given a reference number by the archives office in which they are kept. In the footnotes these follow the name of the office or library. Detailed catalogues of the holdings of Bristol Record Office, Gloucestershire Archives, The National Archives and many other offices are available online, and many original archives and printed sources have been digitized and are also available online. More information about the aims and methods of the Victoria County History will be found on its website.

BIAS Journal	*Bristol Industrial Archaeological Society Journal*
BL	British Library
Bodl. Lib.	Bodleian Library, Oxford
BRO	Bristol Record Office
Cal. Chart.	*Calendar of the Charter Rolls*
Cal. Close	*Calendar of the Close Rolls*
Cal. Pat.	*Calendar of the Patent Rolls*
Dir.	*Directory*
EHR	*English Historical Review*
GA	Gloucestershire Archives
GDR	Gloucester Diocesan Records (at Gloucestershire Archives)
Glos.	Gloucestershire
Glos. Colln.	Gloucestershire Collection (at Gloucestershire Archives)
Glouc.	Gloucester
Glouc. J.	*Gloucester Journal*
HER	Historic Environment Record (available online via Heritage Gateway)
Ibid.	The same as the previous reference or source
Inq. p.m. Glos.	*Abstracts of Inquisitions post mortem for Gloucestershire, 1236–1413, 1625–42* (Six vols. issued jointly by the British Record Soc., Index Library vols. xxx, xl, xlviii, and ix, xxi, xlvii, and the BGAS, 1893–1914)

NHL	National Heritage List for England (https://www.historicengland.org.uk/listing/the-list)
N&Q	*Notes & Queries*
OS	Ordnance Survey
ODNB	*Oxford Dictionary of National Biography* (http://www.oxforddnb.com)
Pers. Comm.	Personal Communication
PN Glos	*The Place-Names of Gloucestershire*, 4 vols. ed. A.H. Smith (1964–5)
Proc. CNFC	*Proceedings of the Cotteswold Naturalists' Field Club*
P.R.S.	Pipe Roll Society
Rec. Com.	Edition published by the Record Commissioners
RO	Record Office
TNA	The National Archives, Kew
Trans. BGAS	*Transactions of the Bristol & Gloucestershire Archaeological Society*, online
VCH	*Victoria County History*, many volumes online via British History Online
Verey and Brooks, *Glos.*	D. Verey and A. Brooks, *Gloucestershire* (Buildings of England) 2 vols. (1999, 2002)
Visit. Glos.	*Visitation of Gloucestershire*
WSA	Wiltshire and Swindon Archives, Chippenham
YHC	Yate History Centre

This is an index of names, places and principal subjects. Places are in Gloucestershire unless otherwise stated, and minor places are in Yate unless otherwise stated.

CPSIA information can be obtained
at www.ICGtesting.com
Printed in the USA
FSHW020534310321
79947FS